NOT YOUR MAMA'S CLASSROOM

Facilitating Engaging, Student-Centered Digital Instruction

DR. WENDY L. OLIVER

TEACHER'S EDITION

LIFEWISE BOOKS

NOT YOUR MAMA'S CLASSROOM

FACILITATING ENGAGING, STUDENT-CENTERED DIGITAL INSTRUCTION

BY DR. WENDY L. OLIVER

Published by:
LIFEWISE BOOKS
PO BOX 1072
Pinehurst, TX 77362
LifeWiseBooks.com

To contact the author | DrWendyOliver.com

ISBN (Print): 978-1-952247-52-1
ISBN (Ebook): 978-1-952247-53-8

DEDICATION

To those of you who have joined me on the journey to improve education for children over the years. Thank you for all you have taught me and for the mentorship and friendship you have provided me along the journey. I look forward to continued learning and our friendships as we continue to innovate and lead change in education for children.

CONTENTS

INTRODUCTION

As the Covid-19 pandemic spread throughout communities across the world, students were sent home from traditional schools. More and more educators began teaching remotely, taking advantage of digital technologies. As the pandemic spiraled, digital programming or remote learning continued as a necessity for many students throughout the 2020-2021 school year. Needless to say, the Covid-19 Pandemic that began in spring of 2020 redefined education throughout the world.

Prior to this sea change in education, I spent two decades of my career leading online and blended learning initiatives. After founding and leading a district-wide online learning program in the 4th largest district in TN, I had the opportunity to found and run Tennessee's first state-led online learning program, e4TN, and later serve as the Chief Learning Architect for Arizona State University's feeder online K-12 program, ASUPD.

Additionally, I have developed frameworks for blended and online instruction as well as an accompanying software for teacher self-assessment of digital pedagogy, served on many national committees impacting digital education in the US, published in academic journals, and published *Not Your Mama's Classroom: What you need to know as a parent about your child's digital education,* in October 2019.

In fall of 2020, I began my podcast series, "Building the Bridge," which is intended to create a bridge between parents and teachers as more and more children participate in digital education.

I was inspired to write *Not Your Mama's Classroom: What you need to know as a parent about your child's digital education,* because over the years, I have observed that we, as an educational community, have not done a good job communicating with parents the needs and expectations we have of them when their children's learning goes online. This has created an educational context in which we have not empowered them to serve in their parental role. Parental support and involvement is critical for success in education. For example, if there is no textbook, how do parents support their children with classwork/homework? Where should the parent go to find examples of how to solve math problems that are assigned for homework without a text to reference?

We don't teach math the same way we did a generation ago. I have an eight-year-old. Trust me. Writing a book that would serve as a resource for parents when their children transition to digital education became a passion project of mine. For as many times as I've complained about a lack of parental involvement, I have been equally guilty of not giving parents the resources they need during their child's digital transition. Now that I'm in the seat of a parent as well, I definitely see areas for growth for communication when children transition to digital education.

Let's fast forward to the 2020 pandemic for which none of us was prepared, obviously. Loads of free digital resources became available to teachers during the initial period of the pandemic. However, educational leaders, to include administrators and providers did not provide adequate professional development for teachers when we required them to begin teaching online, remote, or with 100% digital resources. Not only did we leave adequate training out of the recipe, but our implementation timelines for all stakeholders were not reasonable either. Please note that I'm not criticizing educators, families, students, or educational technology providers during a catastrophic event. What control does anyone have over an act of God? None. We had no other choice but to react and do the best we could, and that is what we did.

A lack of training and condensed timelines for implementation isn't new or isolated to the response to Covid-19. There seems to be a consistent problem with teacher training, timeline, and implementing digital resources. The schools and districts were forced to respond to emergency planning education for during the first months of Covid-19 pandemic. This, coupled with going digital, created what I call remote learning 911. It is important to note that this is not the same model as traditional or effective online or blended learning. We compounded the problem by not providing appropriate training or knowledge of resources for teachers in order to ensure the fidelity of implementation. A lack of parental communication, a condensed timeline, and a lack of teacher training, therefore, created remote learning 911 in spring of 2020, which from some perspectives, was a disaster. For others, it worked well, but I don't believe any teacher would say it was a blissful experience. In short, it was a hot mess, but whether your experience was good or bad, it was definitely a learning experience.

There is a tremendous need for knowledge in the field, but this focus is not on the knowledge parents need around digital learning. Teachers, like parents, need to be empowered with knowledge to support their role in our education community's digital education. Watching Covid-19 unfold, I realized, yet again, I carry a tremendous amount of niche information in my head, but that I only have so much bandwidth. I, again, took to weekends and late nights at the computer in hopes that a book would offer a scalable "self-help" opportunity for teachers. I want teachers to have a resource for their own professional growth as their schools or districts transition to digital instructional models. As I have explained, we are at a sea change in education. We are no longer looking to innovators to lead digital learning. Digital education is no longer the wave of the future; it is part of our everyday education landscape, and it is not going away at this point. For this reason, teachers need to be empowered with knowledge.

With this, I introduce you to *Not Your Mama's Classroom: Facilitating Engaging, Student-Centered Digital Instruction.* The second book in the Not Your Mama's Classroom series is intended to provide teachers with instructional strategies for the digital classroom, to include blended and online. The style of the book is casual and practical with my own classroom stories as well as some of my friends' favorites. Most importantly, it addresses the "how" of digital, not just the "why" or "what."

Whether you are a novice or an experienced online or blended teacher, you will definitely walk away from this book with strategies you can implement immediately. I'd love to know your own ideas and suggestions as well, and I look forward to you communicating them with me to share on my podcast, *Building the Bridge.*

CHAPTER 1

REMOTE LEARNING ENVIRONMENTS

Welcome to teaching in a remote, online, digital, blended, hybrid or even traditional—whatever that is—learning environment. I'd venture to guess you are embarking on a journey to go digital in some form or fashion. I'm hopeful that I can help you on this journey, regardless of the lexicon you, your school, or district is using. Whatever you want to call your new teaching model, the focus of the book is to help you improve your instruction using digital resources and to help you implement your instruction with fidelity.

This means you will have higher levels of student success. Need I say more? Isn't that why we are all in this field? We want to help students find success, and we want to guide them on their journey of learning.

Regardless of why you've gone digital, the biggest advice I can give you is not to give up while you are on this journey, no matter how tempting it might be. Master teachers practice their craft. One study I conducted demonstrated that the majority of novice blended teachers immediately went back to traditional instructional methods as soon as the technology glitched the first time. Before you do this, let me be frank, expect disruption. Teaching with technology won't be perfect. Haven't we all told our students or our own children that we learn from failure?

If you expect disruptions, then it won't be so nerve wrecking when technology does fail, regardless of whether it is user error. Glitchy technology is part of the experience. It builds character! In truth, as optimistic as I want to sound, I completely understand why the teachers in the study I mentioned immediately reverted to paper and pencil. They had 35 students in a classroom. You know, as well as I do, that once you've lost your face-to-face kids' attention (especially if it is a split lunch period), then you are done for the day. Before I can help you with how to prevent technology glitches or how to recover from those glitches, let's discuss the type of digital classroom in which you might be teaching.

TYPES OF DIGITAL CLASSROOMS—HARDWARE

1:1

In this face-to-face classroom, the 1:1 refers to assigning one device per student. In such settings the device can be a tablet, computer, or other mobile device. In this classroom, ideally, you, as the teacher, serve as a facilitator. I'm sure you have been to many professional development seminars, where you were trained to no longer be the "sage on the stage." You may remember your own teachers writing on the board and doing all the talking. This is the type of instruction digital education allows you to avoid. Having access to and implementing a digital curriculum with digital pedagogy allows you to engage learners in activities that are aligned to their individual needs.

In a traditional classroom, you may have up to 35 students or even more. Here you are expected to meet everyone's needs at the same time or teach to the top of the class or the middle, depending on how many students fall into each group of academic ability. This can be very hard, and, as you know, some children get left behind, while others get bored. Finding each child's sweet spot, or "zone of proximal development," if you want to get fancy, also reduces your classroom management issues.

In order to address the breadth of ability in the digital classroom, you may already be implementing "differentiated instruction" to try and meet individual children's needs. With differentiated instruction, each student gets a different assignment based on the child's strengths and/or skills. This requires a lot of advanced preparation, which means you invest a lot of planning time.

In a classroom with advanced technology, you can implement individualized instruction for each student with less planning and preparation, however, because the software will respond or adapt to students' specific needs using artificial intelligence. While one student may need five practice activities to master a concept, another may only need two. There is software that is smart enough to measure whether individual learners need more practice or if they can advance in the learning through an adaptive learning pathway. By the same token, the software can tell if a child may need to practice a skill he or she may not have mastered previously, last year, for example. The software may also be able to tell how a student learns better. In other words, what is an individual's learning preference? With this information, the software could, in theory, "feed" the student content that teaches in the way the child prefers to learn.

In other words, the software may be adaptive. It is a lot like Amazon, Netflix, or Google. Have you noticed how each of these platforms get more accurate at recommending what you might like or in what you might be interested each time you use them? Their recommendation engines use your previous choices as well as compare your interests with those of others like yours to suggest what you might like. Over time, they gather more data, which allows them to become more accurate. This response to your interaction is much like the same adaptive software used in education.

It is important to remember that the level of implementation of the 1:1 model significantly depends on the type of software provided by the district/school, the training you receive, and your comfort with technology. A 1:1 initiative may look very different in classrooms throughout a school or it may be just one component of activities in your classroom as compared to the teacher's classroom next door, who may use it completely differently. Just as students have personalized learning paths, teachers have personalized teaching styles.

In 100% online learning models, sometimes schools provide 1:1 devices for students to take home in order to do their schoolwork. In some face-to-face schools, students are asked to bring in their own devices to do their schoolwork.

BYOD

This sounds like a term we used to refer to parties when I was in college. Well, you are pretty close conceptually. This term actually stands for, "Bring Your Own Device." It can be used in any type of the digital model, and the device can be anything from a tablet to a mobile device. Students are responsible for bringing their own devices to schools and logging into the schools Wi-Fi rather than the school providing devices.

From an instructional perspective, this brings challenges because students may or may not have the same required software downloaded on their personal machines as you expect or require in the classroom or as other students who may be using school-provided machines.

Further, the machines may not have the same requirements for running the software or their capabilities. From a system perspective, IT will be quite busy with protocols to stay ahead of a BYOD model. Beyond the technical concerns, the district will have to implement a program for students on free/reduced lunch who may not have equipment. That said, BYOD doesn't solve all the problems of providing students with computers.

For the most part, in response to Covid-19 there were additional dollars released from the federal government that could be used to purchase, among many things, computers for students. Using funds offered through the 2020 CARES Act, many schools provided 1:1 devices for students. In fact, so many were ordered, some schools still didn't have their devices in November of 2020 due to the increased demand.

However, if you are teaching for an online school where students are using their own machines from home, the school should communicate the minimum technical requirements upon registration. Also, since most software is accessed in the cloud, installing software locally isn't as big of a deal as it used to be.

In a BYOD situation it is important to advise students and families to be familiar with the Acceptable Use Policy (AUP). This is the policy outlining the rules and expectations they must agree to in order to participate or access the school's internet. Students should be signing this each year. You should also have to agree to an Acceptable Use Policy, especially if your school has given you a device to use for your classroom. Teachers, students, and parents should make sure they know which sites or types of sites, such as social media, are restricted under the school's policies.

Internet History

- Regardless of whether students are using 1:1 or BYOD machines, if they take their machines home, they will want to consider Internet history and sites they and their parents are using on their school computer, especially if their parents are using the computer for other purposes such as online purchases or social media. In other words, if a student takes a device to school, with which his or her parent has purchased something online, the student is creating an opportunity for: 1) the parent's identity to be available, which includes the purchasing information, 2) the home location information to be discovered, and 3) the purchase and social media history of the account no matter who used it in the past.

DIGITAL INSTRUCTIONAL MODELS

Before you begin planning your instruction or your curriculum, you have to know the expectations of your administration, even when you are defining your own program. Obviously, if you are in an autonomous setting, you will have your own expectations to decide upon. Either way, let's dive into a few basic models. There are variations and branches of digital education, but if you master or are familiar with the following, then you can easily implement and recognize the others.

Please note that one key factor in your success with the models below is the technology access either provided by the school or by the parent. In most cases, you do not have control over the technology provided to the student. This can make teaching in a digital environment very challenging. When students have appropriate access, digital education can be equally as rewarding as traditional education.

Also, note that each teacher has a different level of comfort and prior knowledge with, not only traditional education, but also with different models and with implementation of each model. Just like with traditional instruction, the more you practice, the more comfortable you become with digital pedagogy, and, therefore, the better digital instructor you become.

Rotation

- Lab Rotation

  The lab rotation model is one of the original models for blended instruction. In this model, teachers take students to a good old fashion computer lab for digital assignments, or teachers bring the lab to students using a mobile computer lab. With CARES funding in 2020, though, many schools are now 1:1, so this model won't be as common. Additionally, as a result of the Covid-19 pandemic, schools are certainly more aware of germs associated with children passing around and sharing devices. Rotating through a computer lab may not currently be an option, but it may be something you are familiar with from previous classroom experience.

- Station Rotation

  Prior to the 2020 pandemic, I suggested all teachers new to blended instruction begin with a station rotation model because it is much like an elementary model, where students work in stations or centers. Most teachers are familiar with this model, and it frees them up to have a center or station to work or conference directly with students while small groups of students work on different activities for a certain number of minutes before rotating. However, during a pandemic or during a post-pandemic era this model is not recommended. Any other time, this model is a great example place to start when implementing blended learning, and many instructors who teach using digital strategies have begun with this model in the past.

It is important to ask yourself, "What are you really trying to do when you 'blend' your instruction?" This answer will, in part, guide your online instructional choices.

TYPES OF DIGITAL CLASSROOMS—INSTRUCTION

Blended

In the blended classroom you "blend" traditional teaching, like you probably had in school, with other strategies that include technology, such as the 1:1 model you just read about. You may choose to have the students rotate in stations with different assignments or use whole class learning. In a blended learning model, with centers a lot like you might see in elementary school, at least one of the centers involves technology. You become a facilitator by integrating technology. In other words, instead of standing in front the classroom and lecturing, ideally, you help as each student progresses through the assignments.

Some components of lessons may still be delivered traditionally, and there is nothing wrong with this. Some lessons or components may, however, be better delivered through the use of technology. The blended classroom takes advantage of the best of both worlds, the traditional and the online mediums, and it allows teachers to individualize learning. In this model it is possible and often likely that students have a personalized learning plan. Just like in the 1:1 model, it is important to remember that the level of implementation of this model varies significantly depending on the teachers' comfort with technology, training, experience, and the software provided.

Be cautious to remember that assigning students to look up something on the Internet and print it off does not mean you have implemented a blended classroom. This is simply called using the Internet. It isn't much different than standing at a copying machine and making a photocopy. In other words, a blended classroom uses the technology as an instructional tool. There are a variety of models of blended instruction. All models, though, include an online component and a face-to-face component. Interaction with, and facilitation by, a talented educator is critical for success in this model. You will need to deeply embed the use of technology into the lesson itself as opposed to using it as a machine or device in order to master a blended classroom.

Flipped

The flipped classroom is a form of the blended classroom that requires a very dedicated student. In theory, this model of the blended classroom allows the students the opportunity to have hands-on interactive practice during the school day with other students, mentors, or the teacher. In order for this model to be successful, the teacher, parent, and student all have to be committed to the model. You, as the teacher, provide "lectures" or teaching through videos that students must view at home the night before or during their free time, so they can practice the skills taught in the online lecture when they attend class.

During the school day, the students work through the problems, which would have traditionally been the homework, that support the practice of learning. This model allows students to have access to the teacher during traditional class time, should they need support or help (rather than at home in the evenings, where no expert in trigonometry is there to provide help). It is similar to when students come in and ask for help with homework. This model alleviates the stress students have from not being able to complete the required homework because the instruction is received at home, while the "homework" is done at school. Technology allows this model of education to be a reality. Because of technology, students receive pre-recorded lectures from their teachers at home the evening before class.

Think about how you might use this model when assigning a group project in order to create more equity among group members. Some students simply *cannot* get together outside of class. Some students simply *will not* get together outside of class. In the flipped classroom, students are responsible for learning the knowledge outside of class time and spending time in the classroom participating in projects or practice during the school day.

The challenge with this model, is that families must agree to do so in advance. Ideally, they sign up for a class or school knowing this is the model. Otherwise, how do students with after-school activities keep up evening academic commitments? If there are older students with jobs, how are they able to keep up if they are working after school? Even if you use this model temporarily, like for a project, for example, it is critical to consider your student population.

Online Classes

The first online school started in 1996 in Massachusetts, so while still a young field, it isn't quite as new as most people think, especially compared to the field of education as a whole. As a matter of fact, there is quite a bit of guidance on what governs a quality online class. There are standards in place, set up by Quality Matters (QM) (2019), National Standards for Quality (NSQ)(2019) and Oliver's Frameworks for Online and Blended Instruction (2014). If you are looking for teaching standards on how digital courses should be designed, best practices exist at: https://qualitymatters.org, https://blendedpractice.com, and/or https://nsqol.org.

An online or virtual class is one where the teacher and student are physically separate, and the course takes place over the Internet. If you are teaching online, you will need to provide a syllabus or course outline for parents and students that explains the course requirements. You will also want to include a pacing guide with due dates for assignments. Usually and, hopefully, there are ways for students to interact with you in an online course such as chat features, email, discussion forums, and/or through your posted office hours. Depending on your program, you may even host a weekly live lesson, where the student can interact with you and one another live or synchronously. Usually, you provide a course calendar equipped with due dates, so parents can help their children manage their time. One of the most challenging aspects of an online class for students is procrastination. Imagine that! I'm sure you've never had to deal with this in a traditional classroom.

Depending on the program, quizzes and tests are either proctored online or in person. Final exams or required state exams usually are required to be taken in person, unless the program works with an online proctoring organization. This requirement, though, depends on the organization, and sometimes you can set this protocol, if they aren't required to be taken in person. Often times, you, as the instructor, can set a password for exams that students are required to enter prior to taking it (you provide it to the student). Sometimes you can set a timer for the exams, assuming the student is provided additional time on his or her IEP. I will go more in depth on strategies for students with exceptional needs in Chapter 6.

ORIENTING PARENTS TO THE DIGITAL LEARNING ENVIRONMENT

In an ideal world, when a school has online classes, the school or online teacher should send home an email, a note, or newsletter explaining the offering(s). The school or teacher should host a parent meeting explaining the type of class(es) and expectations that are set in place for the learning environment. If your class is 100% online, offer a remote or online open house for parents of your students to meet you and learn about your classroom procedures and expectations.

For a blended class, offer some components of your orientation in a blended medium to encourage parents to "try out" the technology and experience these additional features of your classroom. This allows parents to experience the new learning medium you are implementing, so that they will know why you have certain classroom rules that are different from when they went to school.

Even though parents may not attend an open house concept at the school or district-level, this is something you can do in your classroom so that parents can experience the model of learning you are implementing. Unfortunately, I typically see schools implementing wonderful programs but forgetting the key component for success, parents. Instead of "No Child Left Behind," we should make our motto in *digital* education, "No parent left behind."

Parents find it really challenging when their children begin an asynchronous online learning program because students are expected to learn independently and are required to be organized. As an educator, two things should have jumped off the page at you just now. I used the words "independent" and "organized" in the same sentence as "students." Very few students have both of these two characteristics.

Asynchronous learning requires a specific type of learner; one who is a self-starter and typically very organized with good study habits. Quite frankly, this type of student is going to be successful regardless of whether there is a teacher present or not. It is critical if you are teaching in an asynchronous environment to "over-communicate" in order to remain visible and build a rapport with students *and* their parents.

Synchronous classes, on the other hand, include live lessons, which means students can interact with the teacher and one another. They are visible to one another, and this means their conduct can feed off of one another. As a result, there may need to be more classroom rules for behavior. The benefits outweigh the challenges, for there is more opportunity for teacher:student and student:student interaction during group projects in real-time class break-out groups (on video), for example.

Interaction isn't lost in asynchronous (not live) classes, however. Students in an asynchronous class may interact through a discussion board or through peer-edits. Student who are not in real-time classroom contexts benefit from the flexible schedule, time to reflect, and they are not hampered by the physical presence being on video may bring. Because students in a synchronous class regularly "see" the instructor and classmates, instructor visibility, as a critical success factor, is naturally addressed.

USE THE CAMERA RESPONSIBLY

We are social creatures. Because of this, teaching online requires that your students see a human, and that you see humans as well. This only happens with literal visibility. In order to be visible to your students, you will want to discuss and model best practices for the camera on your machine regardless of whether it is yours or the school's.

Let's say you are teaching an online course with a synchronous component, and you are teaching live lessons (See Chapter 6) or even meeting with students on webcam during office hours. In this situation, you should go in and enable the camera on your device when needed.

Other options include removing an inexpensive webcam cover during synchronous instruction, or yet another option to reduce risk is to make sure you don't have the device in a bedroom or other private area, which is always a best practice. There have been situations, where administrators have watched children through webcams of school issued machines, where they suspected activities with drugs, while the children were in the privacy of their homes. In these situations, the administrator may have had good intentions, but a line was crossed. Unfortunately, everyone doesn't always have good intentions. I suggest that knowledge is power when it comes to privacy.

Everything I have described is pertinent to you as an instructor of digital education. It is critical that you model and are able to communicate these best practices with parents as well as students. For example, restricting access to the camera in private settings will prevent a lot of heartache when it comes to social media and oversharing during middle school and high school. The sooner you can implement consistency on your rules for the camera and allowing others into your students' homes digitally, the better.

While we are on the topic of best practices and your camera, please make sure you are protected at home before you take on this new teaching adventure. If you have a router for your wireless internet at home, then it came with a default password. Many times, people don't change the default password to a secure password—one that is private to them. Since brands of routers have common default passwords, people with malicious intentions can hack into your home network by using the default password. Think of it this way. I could drive around your neighborhood and look for the type of router I recognize. When someone malicious does this, he or she can log right into your home through the camera on your computer if you haven't changed the password from the default. Pretty frightening, huh? Let me put this into context. If someone is planning to commit a crime in your home, he could learn your habits and the map of your home through the camera on your computer just by logging into your network, so you need to change that password! If you are teaching blended or online, please advise your families of this too. We are in this together!

CHAPTER 2

TECHNICAL LINGO FOR GOING DIGITAL

You don't have to be a technical expert to teach with digital resources, but it is important that you know the platform your school is adopting, if there is one. This will help you to understand whether you have to remember 15 passwords and user identifications, or if magically all the systems sync with one fabulous user identification such as your email and a password. (We call this Single Sign On or SSO). Understanding more about your school's platform will help you troubleshoot, not only for yourself, but also for your students. A little bit of knowledge can prevent something that is super simple from being extremely frustrating.

The first thing you need know is the delivery system you will be using. Is your district providing a learning management system (LMS)? Some of the more well-known learning management systems in K-12 are Canvas, Blackboard, Desire2Learn, LearningTree, Moodle, Schoology, and Agilix. An LMS is a cloud-based software or platform that offers ways for you to deliver your content. Think of your content as the Thanksgiving dinner, where each dish is one of your classes, and the LMS is the table on which it is served.

Tables come in different shapes and sizes, just as learning management systems come with a variety of functionalities. Most have the capability for you to assess your students, monitor their progress, and track their participation. An LMS usually includes a gradebook; a discussion forum, where you can have asynchronous (not live) discussions amongst students in your class; and a calendar. Most LMS's allow you to create or edit content using a WYSIWYG editor (what you see is what you get), which doesn't require you to know code and an assessment generator, where you can create or use existing assessments for students.

While different learning management systems have their own unique functionalities, they usually all provide an organized way for students to submit their work from locations other than school, and they provide immediate grading. Some systems, such as Learning Tree even provide artificial intelligence or machine learning to assist with student questions, tutoring, teacher grading, or academic integrity. All require teacher interaction for grading of open-ended items.

It is possible for a program, school, or district to implement digital learning without an LMS, and this really depends on the model. For example, if students are participating in a station rotation model, the teacher may not need an LMS to keep them organized or on track. The teacher may only need a software such as IXL. Imagine that a school is just beginning blended learning, and they opt for a station rotation model (much like centers in an elementary classroom). One of the stations the students work in may be a math station, where the students log into the IXL software, rather than an LMS with a teacher created course, for example. This is perfectly acceptable.

In a software program such as IXL, the system maintains each student's analytics in a dashboard with views for both the teacher, parent, and the student. The predictive analytics recommend lessons based on each student's performance, and the data is visible to the teacher and parent.

There is no need for an LMS in this station rotation example. This is also why it is critical to know the vision of the school and the model you are being asked to implement.

What if you are being asked to implement an online course, but you aren't given a curriculum that is a completely developed course like an FLVS, EdisonLearning, or Accelerate course, for example? Whether you like the way these content providers organize their content or not, the fact that everything is in one place does make life easier for you and for the students. If presented with disparate resources, students often don't know where to go to find the next activity.

Let's say you are provided with miscellaneous resources that the district has licensed for a fictitious math course you are building. You and the students, for example, have licenses, provided by the district, to IXL Math, Carnegie Math, Aleks Math, and Math Media as your content resources, and you have to create your course from scratch using these providers. Rather than having your students lost and trying to explain which resource to log into daily or within the lesson, ideally, your IT or LMS manager will implement single sign on (SSO) with your LMS. With SSO, learners use just one user ID and one password, typically through their LMS, to authenticate all the sites you plan to use when teaching. SSO avoids a lot of headaches in the long run because the number one IT question in digital education is, "What is my user ID?" or "What is my password?" If you plan to link out to a few sites here and there, then, of course, there is no need to include SSO, but if your curriculum is based on multiple sites, then, by all means, if you have the IT team to support you, I suggest you ask for SSO.

Speaking of SSO, many schools or districts use Google Classroom. Do you know that most learning management systems can integrate with Google Classroom? In this scenario, once you and/or students sign into Google Classroom, they will see an app/logo for the LMS. From here they can launch their LMS. There are so many ways to make the digital learning experience smooth and easy for teachers and students. Nobody needs an additional password to remember. I know I sure don't! I do realize that some of you are using Google Classroom as your LMS, but it isn't technically an LMS. It does not have a gradebook and you cannot automate users within it. Additionally, while you can post PowerPoints and other types of content in it, it isn't really designed to be a content management system. So, depending what your school or program's vision is you may need to integrate with an LMS as well as use Google Classroom.

There are other platforms that are content management systems (CMS) that you may be using such as Edgenuity. A CMS, typically, is specific to a product and is designed to manage a unique course style or individual company's content, whereas, an LMS is designed to be more generic and host anybody's content. So, you might be teaching on an LMS, a CMS, just using a specific software, a live feed with Zoom or another live stream, or any variety of ways. The key is to understand the vision of the administration or leadership for whom you are working and to understand the best way to engage the learners you have the privilege to serve.

Please notice that I talked about licensed software in this chapter. Many of the so-called "free" educational resource sites have terms buried or hidden in their privacy policies or terms of use stating that they aren't responsible for how their 3rd party partners use the data from cookies on your device once you or a student creates a user account. Too many times I've seen teachers ask students to create accounts without parental permission. Why does this matter? It is for school, right?

a) There is a requirement for parental permission by the website.

b) Personal data is collected by the website.

Certainly, teachers don't know student data or even their own data is shared with 3rd parties, but you have to remember that "free" is never really free. Granted, most teachers have not been sufficiently trained in online resources, which is why I'm so grateful you have invested in your continued learning through this resource. We have to be knowledgeable of reputable sources and when we are asking families to give away Personally Identifiable Information (PII) in exchange for a free resource. You also need to know when you are giving away your own data. As tempting as it is to just check the "Terms of Use" box when you are signing up for something, your data is too valuable, as is a student's, even if the website or resources could be a great teaching tool. I'm sorry to say, but you actually need to read all that legal gobbledygook in the terms of use before agreeing to anything.

CHAPTER 3

EVALUATING DIGITAL CURRICULUM

If you've gone digital, and your school provided digital content, then congratulations! You are one of the lucky ones. In some instances, teachers are responsible for creating their own digital curriculum for blended or online learning courses from scratch. As I mentioned in earlier chapters, this is often expected to be accomplished with no digital resources and very little, if any, training provided.

This sounds pretty crazy, right? Well, it is more common than you think. After all, teachers are jacks of all trades, correct? At least, I always thought my teachers knew everything, right?!

The bad news is that even when your district or school provides you with digital content, it isn't always aligned 100% to course objectives and/or state standards. On top of this, students may need additional practice that isn't provided for or by the digital product.

In my experience, I have yet to see a curriculum product that meets all of my expectations, which is bad because I design digital products now. Where I see the real gap; however, is in training. A provider may have the most beautiful product in the world, but if teachers receive one four-hour training session on it, they won't be able to implement it with fidelity. Much like a surgeon learning to implement a new procedure, teachers need additional training in order to effectively implement digital curriculum and instruction. This training needs to be more than where to point and click on the screen or a two-hour session on how wonderful the company is. Going digital is a complete pedagogical shift, so a two-hour webinar just won't do the trick. In reality, teachers don't have the time to truly invest in learning products inside and out, and many are burnt out on trainings and professional development. The good news is that by investing your time now you are beginning your own journey to grow your knowledge of digital education. You will have the pedagogical knowledge of the medium even if you only receive a two-hour product training or the training you received was not helpful.

One of the benefits of going digital is that when you need to find curriculum to supplement classroom content, be it online or face-to-face, there is a wealth of resources. This is true even if the digital resources are provided. However, this creates additional work and requires new skills and knowledge for teachers. I hear you! Who needs more work?

Think of it like this. In your face-to-face classroom, you cannot pick up a textbook and meet every students' needs by following the suggested curriculum. Out of instinct, I'm sure you pull curriculum from a variety of resources. Much like this scenario, when digital curriculum is provided by a vendor, teachers may still need to find and add resources to meet the needs of all of their learners.

STANDARDS FOR DIGITAL CURRICULUM

There are national standards that you can use as a guide for evaluating different K-12 digital courses. The International Association for

Online Learning (iNACOL) created the first set of standards for K-12 online programs in 2007. iNACOL, now called the Aurora Institute, supported efforts in 2019, of experts from across the United States and Canada, who were organized by Virtual Learning Leadership Alliance and Quality Matters, to update the previous standards. I had the fortunate opportunity to help lead this initiative. The work of the teams of experts resulted in three updated sets of standards, to include the National Standards for Quality Online Courses (2019). NSQ Quality Online Course standards include seven standards arranged from A-G. The standards will be updated every three years and can be found at www.nsqol.org/the-standards:

Standard A	Course Overview and Support
Standard B	Content
Standard C	Instructional Design
Standard D	Learner Assessment
Standard E	Accessibility and Usability
Standard F	Technology
Standard G	Course Evaluation

Each standard has a set of indicators, along with explanations and examples, which are particularly helpful as you implement the standards, not just evaluate online courses. Included with these standards are explanations and examples.

For example:

> Standard A1 states: "A course overview and syllabus are included in the online course."

Explanations: An overview of the course and the syllabus make clear to learners how to get started and where to find essential course components. These can be presented up front in the course instructions.

Example: The instructor has a syllabus posted in the course that includes a scope and sequence, pacing guide, contact information, link to orientation, textbook information, and grading information.

Using the example from Standard A1, while you may review vendor products to determine if they have a course overview and syllabus, as an instructor, it is critical to make these resources visible to students in your online course. In the example above, the instructor is provided with specific details as to how to make the course overview and syllabus accessible and useful for students. You will find that these documents are equally as important for your planning and organization.

Another set of standards that will help you as you evaluate online courses is available from Quality Matters (QM) (2019), an organization that was started by Maryland Online, Inc. The original goal of the group of colleagues was to determine how to measure the quality of an online course. This could be exactly what you need, especially since, QM is the leader in quality assurance in online courses. QM provides two applicable rubrics, one for vendor courses and one for courses developed by K-12 institutions (your state's virtual school, district, or school created content).

Obviously, if your school or district is providing you courses from a for-profit content provider, then the vendor rubric should apply when evaluating them. Vendors have the opportunity to earn certification from QM on their courses. If the course you are reviewing is QM certified, then you can trust that it meets the QM standards for best pracitices. If the course is not certified, then you can apply the QM rubric as you evaluate it to determine quality.

What should you expect from a vendor course?

If you have never taught online before, what expectations should you have of a vendor created course so that you can get organized and begin implementing best practices of digital instruction? Further, how do you make it your own since you cannot exactly put up bulletin boards like you do in the traditional classroom?

A vendor course should have several resources included in the teacher materials that will make your life easier. For example, you should always expect that a syllabus and a pacing guide are provided for you and the students. A syllabus will outline the entire course for you, so you (and students and parents) will know the requirements of the class. It should also tell you the minimum technological requirements to run the content, so that you can make sure you have the ability to download all the required software.

You can also determine if the grading criteria is to your preference based on how it is presented in the syllabus. Then you can personalize the syllabus with content such as contact information, office hours and communication preferences. If you change the grade weighting, don't forget to update the syllabus. A curriculum alignment should also be included. This will indicate where in the content each standard is taught and how it is assessed.

Most platforms allow administrators to set an automatic pace for students based on their start and end dates, which is determined during the enrollment process. Let's say Elizabeth starts her nine-week class two weeks late because she was competing at Nationals. A pacing guide will automatically modify her schedule of assignments so that she will complete it in seven weeks rather than nine. She would have more work each day in order to complete the class on time if her end date is the same as the other students enrolled in the section.

Even if administration sets the pacing guide, you should expect one in order to plan accurately in the teacher materials or course resources. A pacing guide will tell you the approximate time you should expect for students to complete each assignment. If the course is mastery-based, though, you will have to keep in mind that all students may not be required to do the same or all activities. Your institution should have a set predetermined mastery score for mastery-based courses. For example, if the institution sets the mastery score at 80%, then students must earn an 80% on an assessment in order to move forward to new content. You will want to make sure the mastery-based course settings align to the requirements of your institution.

Just because your school/district provided digital content for you, doesn't mean you have it easy. Albeit you have it much easier than if you were developing your course from scratch. A few questions you want to ask yourself are:

- Will your students be prepared either for the end of course exam or the next level based on the content/alignment provided? If the answer is no, then you will need to supplement.
- Does the online course meet the specific requirements of your institution? For example, are all students required to do a capstone? Given your students' home environment, are the real-world activities provided in the curriculum reasonable, or do you need to substitute?
- Depending on the platform for your digital content, you or your institution will need to decide if you want passwords to be required before exams will open.

- Do you want to proctor assessments online by having students on camera when they test? Or does the software come with a proctoring tool?
- Will students be required to progress chronologically in the digital curriculum, view every file and document, or can the students complete assignments out of a set order?
- This is an important decision because if you don't require custom pathways, sometimes called conditional releases, then students may skip the actual content and just complete the required assignments. You read that correctly, they won't read the content or do the practice activities. They will jump directly to the assessments to try and rush through the course.
- You may also want to create groups of students in your online classroom. This will make it easier if you need to assign specific resources to certain groups of students. You can also use these groups for collaboration, grading, or communication. It is quicker and easier to select a group of students to send an email rather than individually emailing each student. Be sure to create the groups with intent and don't just randomly select who will be with whom.

Even if your school/district provides digital curriculum for you as a resource, you may still want to supplement or provide personalized activities for students, especially if Response to Intervention (RTI) resources or real-world connections are not included in the provided digital curriculum.

CHAPTER 4

ENGAGING STUDENTS IN DIGITAL CURRICULUM

Recently, I had a chance to speak on a panel, where I was asked for examples of how students were being engaged through remote and online learning. This is a common question, but it is one that always requires further clarification, for involvement in the school community is often referred to as engagement. Examples for this include, students participating in activities to monitor and maintain the school culture or engaging in such a way that their own social and emotional learning (SEL) is being addressed.

Engagement activities for school culture might include activities such as dressing out of uniform for pajama day, which can be seen in live meetings, or encouraging school-based clubs or committees to meet via remote options. Other examples include opportunities for interacting with other learners for social engagement such as scheduled lunch meetings or one-on-one student-teacher collaborations on Zoom, Google Meet, or various other streaming platforms. In a 100% online environment, special attention has to be given to meet SEL needs of students. Schools focus on live counseling services, gaming software,

software monitoring, and a variety of other methods to support the social and emotional needs of children. The key is to provide social opportunities for students to interact and for educators to monitor the well-being of learners.

DEVELOPING THE MATERIAL

When most people think of online classes, they assume students are not as engaged as they are in the face-to-face classroom. However, digital curriculum can be more engaging than face-to-face instruction. Learners can be more motivated than with traditional learning. There can be more collaboration with the instructor than in person, and there can be an increased learning and understanding of subject matter (Coomey & Stephenson, 2001). The best part is that all of this can happen when you are in your sweatpants or jammies. Too good to be true? Well, remember, 100% asynchronous online learning isn't for every child, just like face-to-face instruction isn't for every child. Interacting with digital resources is a necessity in order for students to be prepared for the workforce. Implementing a variety of instructional strategies in your digital curriculum will help students be more successful, not only in their academic studies but also in college or career. So, whether you are teaching blended, hybrid, or online, there is an absolute need to implement and design digital curriculum, even though the implementation may vary.

It is easy to give students a multiple-choice test in an online class, even better, it will be automatically graded. However, implementing authentic assessments, as we will discuss in the next chapter, engages students more than simply using multiple choice tests or quizzes. Let's go a step further. If you have students collaborate on their authentic assessments, then you will reap the benefits of your instructional design, for students will construct their own knowledge. They will also develop technology skills that will help with their employability. True learning occurs when students actually think, not as a result of a slideshow or PowerPoint presentation in an online classroom (It's a good thing this book isn't written for higher ed, or I might have just offended someone). When students make connections from the curriculum to the real-world, they are more likely to remember what they learn (Brown, Roediger, McDaniel, 2014).

The good news is that the online medium is ideal for a student-centered learning experience, where students are at the center of instruction rather than the teacher. This is the opposite of the Charlie Brown teacher, if you are old enough to remember her. In this model, the teacher in the role of the sage on the stage is no more, and because of student engagement with the digital curriculum, they take responsibility for their own learning. A learner-centered strategy is effective online because students can connect to the content through a variety of ways. Since, in a learner-centric classroom, students learn based on their own skills or goals, differentiated instruction is a given. Individual needs of students are recognized along with their various interests.

While you may employ a learner-centered approach in your face-to-face classroom, because of the nature of the digital classroom, which includes personalized learning paths, flexible scheduling, and pacing, thereby encouraging one-on-one interaction, it is easier for online teachers to diversify instruction and personalize interactions with students in the online classroom. For example, if the platform you are using allows, you can have students take a pre-assessment, and the platform, in many cases, will customize students' learning paths. This means you don't have to spend time planning out differentiated instruction for each student.

There are other ways to create a learner-centered classroom without diagnostic assessments and customized learning paths, though. One instructional method that is ideal for online learning is project-based learning (PBL). This method truly personalizes learning. Students are collaboratively engaged in solving a real-world problem, and they have to be self-directed in their work to successfully complete a PBL. Although, access to technology determines the way in which students collaborate at a distance, the instructional strategy of having students collaborate is what drives motivation and engagement, thereby increasing learning.

Big picture, though, regardless of the method, (be it project-based learning, problem-based learning, experiential learning, whole-group instruction, cooperative learning...), according to Rice (2012, p. 27) "effective online instruction" promotes:

1. Learner autonomy
2. Active participation
3. Collaboration and community building
4. Authentic assessment
5. Acquisition of 21st century skills

As you well know, you can only accomplish these five characteristics with your online instruction if the course or content is designed in a way that encourages these traits for learners. As you think about your online curriculum or even an online course that you have taken, does it meet the five characteristics above as described by Rice (2012)? What are some strategies you can incorporate when you create your digital content, or what are strategies that you can implement with vendor or curated resources to increase the effectiveness of your digital content?

Learner Autonomy

Learner autonomy is a learner's ability to be in control of or take charge of his or her own learning, and this significantly impacts achievement. How can you achieve this in your online class? So much about online learning is autonomous just by its very nature, even before you begin to implement your own learning strategies. Students, in many ways have control over their own destinies when they log into their own independent learning model, where their learning can be personalized or customized, where pacing may be at their own discretion, where they may be allowed flexibility in their work location, where they may no longer have to follow a school dress code... By adding learning strategies to give them a sense of control over how they learn, you increase their success in this new learning model, where they can define what success looks like in their own independent way.

Are you wondering how you can have an autonomous classroom that is also interactive? Online, of course. What else would you expect me to say at this point? By taking advantage of some of the tools online, you can have an active and collaborative classroom, even an asynchronous one, that also provides learner autonomy. Striking the right balance of these qualities is what makes the most effective digital classroom. You can do this by getting to know your students by asking them their goals, interests, or hobbies. Try sending out a survey at the beginning of the year/semester or by asking students to complete an "All about me" survey. For younger students, you can ask them to record and upload their hobbies or interests. You can also accomplish learner autonomy in an online class or with digital resources pretty intuitively, especially if you use methods like a project-based-learning, where students can drive the outcome of the project, and there is no one-size-fits all for the outcome.

Another way to encourage learner autonomy is by providing options and allowing students to select their own learning resources. In some cases, you can provide different opportunities based on learning preference, for example. Ask students to further their own learning by seeking out additional information in order to make connections, or you can simply ask younger students to make personal connections and submit them via audio file, mp3 file, video, or written submissions, if age appropriate.

Don't forget to ask students to set goals and reflect on their learning (Hattie, 2009). This is critical for metacognition and continued engagement. You can set up remote rooms for students to collaborate and work together based on their own interests or skill levels. I have seen this done in a "live lesson" (See chapter 6), where students collaborated, reflected, and made connections to learning with peers. It was really cool to see.

If there isn't a synchronous opportunity through a live feature, these same concepts can be done in a discussion forum, Google Classroom, or even email, if you don't have a robust platform. Although the 2020 Covid-19 pandemic caused many teachers to jump into remote online instruction very quickly and overwhelmingly, I am impressed to see the level of interaction and implementation of synchronous interactivity through breakout rooms in Zoom and similar tools. Students are able to work in cooperative learning groups and peer edit or collaborate on projects, albeit at a distance, much like professionals do in their careers. By the way, you might consider using online collaboration tools with other teachers to share resources. They don't even have to be teachers who are physically in your school district!

For older students, self-pacing and independent learning lend themselves to online learning and are a given when designing for learner autonomy. Learner autonomy actually encourages critical thinking, so if you can nail this, then you also nail a 21st century skill.

Active Participation

Have you taken an online course where all you did, literally, was read and answer questions either in the discussion board or as an assignment?

I know you are shocked to learn that passive methods are not the most effective ways to learn in an online class or with digital resources. The idea is *not* to put students on a remote island isolating them with the curriculum or digital resources where they passively read to pass the time required to get a grade. Students need to be a part of the learning. By providing opportunities for students to be self-directed and remain engaged, you are well on your way to a learning environment where students are participating actively.

Students can be set up to work in cooperative learning groups, for example, which can be done using break out rooms with synchronous tools. You can do this and assign students roles like you would in the physical classroom. Have a student be the reporter, for example. This would report out the group's findings when the class reconvenes, or the reporter could post the group's conclusion in the discussion forum. Another student might be the researcher; another could be the secretary; and another could be the artist. These roles obviously vary depending on the assignment and students. As you can imagine, taking on these roles could be quite intimidating, so it is critical that you, as the instructor, build an individual rapport with each student. Remember the "All about me" survey? This will provide you with details you can use to reach out to individual students or to group students based on interest and resources available to them at home. They are smart cookies, so I have no doubt they will figure out that you are making time to take their interests into consideration.

Group Work

If you are grouping students for project work, and you are operating on a traditional school calendar for enrollment, then collaborative activities can be great. If you, however, are teaching in a model where the program has rolling enrollment (where students can enroll at any time) then activities where students collaborate with one another may not be as easy to pull off. This is where asynchronous communication comes in handy. I have seen students who are shy, or even students who are less academically talented, develop and grow tremendously when using asynchronous online tools because they have the opportunity to have more "think time," or because they can research before making a final declaration. Students don't have to collaborate with one another in order to be actively engaged. They can also interact with the content and with you.

Collaboration and Community Building

It may seem like it is harder to build community in an online classroom or when your students are using digital resources, but you just have to think outside the box. Some similarities with creating community in the traditional classroom include but are not limited to class rules, student:student and student:teacher rapport, and setting expectations. To encourage community in your online class, ask students with related interests to work on service-oriented projects. This can be done through a discussion forum, live room, physical meet up, or even in a chat. You should reach out to students using a variety of tools. You may reach out electronically or even by voice, in order to create a collaborative community. Another way to collaborate and create community is by assigning a class project and awarding points to teams for specific tasks. These activities will encourage your students to interact with you and others.

When I ran Tennessee's online learning program, e4TN, I worked with a student who was extremely far behind academically. The school decided to try putting the student in online classes, in hopes that he might be more successful online than he was in person. The student was so successful that the school's leadership asked him to oversee their face-to-face computer lab. A form of community building for the student was that he was in a leadership role as an official lab supervisor. By the way, the student ended up catching up on his credits through online classes, and he graduated!

INCENTIVES AND GAMIFICATION

How do you incentivize a student that you cannot see in person? It is much easier online than in person, and you don't have to stay up all night baking cookies for students like I did my first year of teaching. Can I get an "Amen" to that?

As a matter of fact, some platforms are gamified and do the work for you, which definitely interests the edutainment generation. Can you say, "Hello, Pavlov"? With purchased digital curriculum, you will typically find gamification or incentives to keep students engaged like badges, points, levels, and other game-based motivators. For example, as students complete work, they may earn points, and badges may be released. These badges can be tied to level of difficulty or progress in the course or any variety of metrics. Progress in the course as it relates to the pacing (are assignments being submitted on time, early, or late) may determine if the student receives incentives to help him or her advance in a game. The goal, of course, is to encourage the student to advance in the content in order to earn resources to play the game.

If you don't have a software or curriculum that has gamification or incentives built in, then how can you create your own incentive program for online or blended students? Many of your options depend on the model of the program for which you are designing classes, but I will provide some example ideas. Teachers, by nature are very creative people, especially when it comes to free. I have no doubt you either have or will come up with some awesome ideas.

Free Ideas

Students can earn:

- A homework pass
- The chance to do even/odd rather than all homework problems
- The chance to view an exam early
- The chance to drop a quiz grade
- Extra credit
- An opportunity to choose teacher hair style
- An opportunity to be the teacher for a period of time
- A chance to host a pet parade
- A chance to pick the music/YouTube video to play at lunch or break

ACQUISITION OF 21ST CENTURY SKILLS

I'm sure you've heard that you have a responsibility to prepare students for the 21st century global economy. You will note that many of the traits for effective online learning include these skills.

Four skills necessary for the 21st include:

- Critical Thinking
- Creativity
- Collaboration
- Communication

Other 21st century skills include digital literacy, leadership, flexibility, and others. At the core of these competencies, if students master the four C's, as referenced above, then they will be more successful in college and in their careers. A distinct trait of effective online content, creativity, is common in authentic assessments, as well. Depending on the design of the lesson, these traits, for the most part, overlap. In another example, consider active participation and collaboration or learner autonomy and collaboration. It isn't necessary to think of the five traits in isolation. Rather, when designing your online content, focus on instructional activities that meet most or all of them.

CHAPTER 5

DESIGNING YOUR DIGITAL CURRICULUM & ALIGNING YOUR ASSESSMENTS

Teaching with digital resources is a new, flexible experience and requires different skills than the traditional classroom, which means the initial transition to teaching with digital tools will be an investment of your time. Remember being a first-year teacher? Okay—it isn't that bad. However, if your school or district doesn't provide packaged or vendor-created curriculum, then not only do you have to learn a new pedagogy, but you will have to develop your own curriculum too. There are a variety of ways to do this, from curating online resources, to writing all of your own content from scratch.

The good news is that once you have a solid foundation, each time you teach the course, it will be much easier, ultimately ending with you facilitating student-learning. Also, as teachers, we are trained to teach curriculum, not to develop it. This is why, in most cases, face-to-face teachers do not develop their curriculum from scratch. The school or district typically provides resources that can and may even be required to be used in the classroom, or teachers fund their own curriculum (because they make so much money).

While the majority of classroom resources are not necessarily paper-based anymore, the actual design of the resources has been done for teachers. This does save time and allows the teacher to focus more on the facilitation of the resources than the development.

For the teacher who does not have curriculum provided, and has to design his or her digital content, there are a host of additional and different considerations and requirements for the digital medium and environment. As mentioned in the previous chapter, there are standards that you can follow as you design your course or digital resources. Please note, especially perfectionists, I don't suggest you try to tackle all of the standards right out of the gate. However, familiarizing yourself with them will definitely help as you grow your expertise, the quality of your digital resources, and the level of engagement of your students in your digital course.

BEGIN AT THE BEGINNING

So, now that you have the big picture of the traits of effective digital curriculum, how do you roll up your sleeves and start planning for your new digital class? Where do you begin? It may not surprise you that "good instruction is good instruction," so there really isn't that much difference in the planning or design phase of digital content verses face-to-face. As a matter of fact, when designed correctly, digital instruction can be as or more effective for student learning than face-to-face instruction (Oliver, 2010; Roblyer and Doering, 2013).

There are, of course, variables involved in creating an impactful digital learning experience because, depending on the model, students approach and interact with the curriculum much differently online than in the traditional classroom. If you are teaching in a blended format or curating resources for a blended model, you may not need to focus as much on overall digitally focused design, but if you are developing curriculum for a completely online course, synchronous or asynchronous, you will definitely need to give special attention to your design.

ACKNOWLEDGING DIFFERENCES RELEVANT TO DESIGN

What are some of the differences? In a face-to-face classroom, teachers rely quite a bit on their personalities and discussions to create "engagement." Having students work in groups face-to-face is another way that teachers engage them in face-to-face classroom collaborative activities. While collaboration is critical to an effective online course, it is essential to remember that online students do not have peers sitting next to them to do fun group activities or collaborate, unless you count the family pet. This is why Chapter 4 is focused on engagement ideas for learner-to-learner and learner-to-teacher collaboration.

Another differentiator between the teaching environments is the removal of face-to-face interaction for communicating expectations with students. I often observe new online teachers not providing clear enough instructions or rubrics with enough detail for online students. Consider that many students do not read and follow directions well to begin with, and the combination results in the plummeting effectiveness of a digital course. Your visibility and organization as an online teacher truly impact the success of each student.

Of course, you are still required to meet the requirements of a student's 504 or an IEP, but obviously, when using digital resources, accessibility is a whole new world. Meeting requirements for students with exceptional needs takes on a completely different set of requirements (See chapter 6) when using digital resources and not physically being in person. Don't let these or other differentiations in the online environment deter you from taking on the challenge of teaching digitally, for there are many benefits to the digital classroom as well.

With digital resources, the technology can immediately drive personalization of the curriculum, reducing the teacher's planning time and allowing you to spend more one-on-one time with students. In these situations, students benefit from individualized curriculum that is dependent upon their performance or mastery. As previously discussed, many technology platforms automatically recommend additional practice for students when they are struggling to master a skill or standard if the technology senses that students are struggling to perform. I spent hours assessing students and locating resources in my face-to-face classroom in order to provide this level of personalization. How about you? This time savings alone was enough to motivate me to transition to and design my own digital resources.

Remember the incentives from Chapter 4? The good news is that you can design your digital content and even include incentives in such a way that students can be engaged without you having to take night classes on how to write code, machine learning, statistics, or even culinary classes.

PLANNING AND DESIGNING YOUR ONLINE COURSE

It's time to put on your thinking caps and grab a cup of coffee because the rest of this chapter will focus on curriculum and assessment design. Or perhaps you are an oddball like me, and you love digging in and working on the details? In that case, grab your popcorn because we are about to have some fun.

Let's review Education 101 and then some... Remember Bloom's Revised Taxonomy? What about Norman Webb's Degrees of Knowledge? I'm going to jolt your memory a little because learner engagement is truly based on the higher levels of both of these taxonomies or frameworks, as is rigor. Rigor is a very debated topic, especially in online classes. In an online class or with digital resources, it is critical that you engage students with rigorous activities. Otherwise, the success rates in your online course will suffer. Note the redundancy in engaging students with rigorous activities in the previous sentences. A rigorous course isn't defined as hard. It is defined as engaging.

During the design phase of developing your online curriculum or resources, just like in the face-to-face environment, you have to make sure that state standards are taught and assessed. Students have to be appropriately prepared for the end of course (EOC) assessments and/or the next grade level. While there is a place for them, if all your digital resources align to Bloom's level one, or Webb's DOK one, then students will not be engaged, nor will your digital curriculum be rigorous. Your students won't be able to do much more than recall or remember the information presented. This also means your student success rates will likely be low. I know you don't want that, so let's determine how you make curriculum rigorous for all students.

Bloom's Revised Taxonomy

Bloom's Revised Taxonomy is a taxonomy for measuring cognitive rigor in teaching, learning, and assessment, and is often used in instructional settings. If you recall, the original framework focused on nouns; however, the revised taxonomy (2001) focuses on verbs that help educators determine the level of cognitive complexity (thinking) associated with a student expectation.

So, how do you use this taxonomy during the design phase to help make your online class engaging?

In the design phase of your online course you create your curriculum map and align your lesson targets with your objectives, which, of course, align with your standards. This is how you guarantee that you are teaching all of the required standards. Sound familiar? Remember, good instruction is good instruction, so a lot of this information carries over from the traditional classroom too. Just like in the face-to-face setting, once you have deconstructed your standards, it is easy to add your objectives and learning targets. In order to do this accurately and align student expectations, it is critical that you apply, Bloom's Revised Taxonomy framework or Webb's Degrees of Knowledge not only to instructional objectives and student learning targets but also to the alignment of assessment strategies. Otherwise, you could teach students a standard at a low level, like a level one on Bloom's, and turn around and assess them at a level five (Chappuis, J., Stiggins, R., Chappuis, S., Arter, J. 2012; Rice, 2012; Sheninger & Murray, 2017). This would be like coaching the championship basketball game of the season with a team that you never had practice with prior to the game.

Deconstructing Standards

Deconstructing standards allows you to identify the cognitive processes (level of thinking) or the level of Bloom's or level of Webb's the standard expects the student to master. After deconstructing the standard in order to determine the objectives, which should each contain a noun and a verb, the curriculum developer or teacher can align the level of cognitive processes a learner needs to encounter when interacting with the new knowledge.

How hard does the student have to think? The learner should then experience a cognitive process dimension, which is a continuum of increasing cognitive complexity, a fancy way to say scaffolding, throughout a course (Chappuis, J., Stiggins, R., Chjappuis, S., Arter, J., 2012).

Boy that was a mouthful, but think of it like this:

> When I trained for the marathons I ran, I didn't run 26.2 miles for my initial training. I slowly worked up to my final goal, starting with five miles as my long run for the week and concluding with 22 miles for my longest run of the week over a 16-week period. Learning applies the same concept of building up your endurance over time, and we refer to this as scaffolding.

Using my marathon analogy, if I trained accordingly, I would successfully complete my run of 26.2 miles. Talk about a true performance assessment! Similar to the marathon and the training I had, with curriculum, the assessment strategies should be aligned to the deconstructed standard. This also means that you should purposely align to the same level of Bloom's Revised Taxonomy or Webb's Degrees of Knowledge as the objectives and learning targets.

Let's revisit my marathon analogy.

> My goal was to run 26.2 miles; therefore, my assessment is to run 26.2 miles. The level of difficulty should align seamlessly. For example, my first marathon was in Nashville, and the course was full of hills. This means if I didn't train running hills, then I would not have been prepared for the marathon and likely not met my goal.

So how do you put all this magic together to create engaging or rigorous online curriculum? It is kind of like making your great grandmother's famous apple pie. You follow a recipe, and each time you "cook up" a digital course it gets better.

Let's go through the whole process of applying Bloom's Revised Taxonomy, deconstructing a standard, and determining lesson learning targets for a Common Core standard. In other words, let's follow the recipe to create a curriculum map.

Bloom's Revised Taxonomy is made up of six categories of cognitive complexity. Within each category, there are verbs to help instructors and curriculum developers classify the level of cognitive processes the student is experiencing while mastering a learning target. In other words, each level addresses the question: How hard does the learner have to actually think in order to complete the task? The higher the number, the more complex the thought process (Chappuis, J., Stiggins, R., Chappuis, S., Arter, J. 2012; Rice, 2012; Sheninger & Murray, 2017).

BLOOM'S REVISED TAXONOMY LEVELS

1. Remember: Students identify and remember information (recognize, recall…).
2. Understand: Students interpret, exemplify, classify, summarize, compare, and explain (paraphrase, translate, clarify, categorize, conclude, predict, compare/contrast, match…).
3. Apply: Students execute and implement (construct, determine, discover, investigate, predict).
4. Analyze: Students differentiate and organize (classify, explain, compare, identify, outline…).
5. Evaluate: Students verify or check and critique (assess, conclude, interpret, predict…).
6. Create: Students generate, plan, and produce (categorize, formulate, develop, create, summarize…).

Example using Bloom's Revised Taxonomy

Common Core Standard: CCSS.ELA-Literacy.RL.9-10.2
Determine a theme or central idea of a text and analyze in detail its development over the course of the text, including how it emerges and is shaped and refined by specific details; provide an objective summary of the text.

Now for the fun stuff! Let's actually deconstruct the standard. First identify any key terms the students will need to know and understand in order to master the standard.

KEY TERMS:

- theme
- objective summary

Then identify all the *actions* the standard requires the student to do.

ACTIONS:

- Determine a theme
- Determine a central idea of text
- Analyze the theme over the course of the text
- Analyze how the theme emerges
- Analyze how the theme is shaped and refined by specific details
- Provide an objective summary of the text

Check this out! All of these actions are now the objectives you need to teach in order to appropriately teach the standard. Notice each one begins with a verb.

- The learner will be able to: <u>determine</u> a theme or central idea of text.

- The learner will be able to: analyze the theme over the course of the text.
- The learner will be able to: analyze how the theme emerges in the text.
- The learner will be able to: analyze how the theme is shaped and refined by specific details from the text.
- The learner will be able to: provide an objective summary of the text.

What do you notice about the underlined verbs above? Yes! Each verb is from level four of Bloom's. Obviously, this wasn't accidental. So, I might choose to teach this standard with the following objective, which you will note is consistently aligned to Bloom's level four. Sorry math and science teachers.

OBJECTIVE:

The learner will be able to determine a theme or central idea of a text by comparing themes from Dr. Martin Luther King's, "Letter from Birmingham Jail" with *Antigone.*

Learning Targets

There is one more step to go to put this in words students can understand that also gives them autonomy. Remember, objectives are for teachers. *Learning targets are for students,* and they give students a goal or target, like my marathon goal did for me. They are also written in student friendly language. A student can read a learning target and know exactly what he or she will be able to do upon completion of the unit. Ideally, overarching learning targets, defined in chunks, are then broken down further into daily or lesson targets, like my weekly training runs (Chappuis, J., Stiggins, R., Chappuis, S., Arter, J. 2012;

Rice, 2012; Sheninger & Murray, 2017). The student then owns the learning rather than the teacher, and the student knows exactly what is required of him or her.

Learning Target: I can compare/contrast how Dr. Martin Luther King and Antigone use nonviolent civil disobedience to challenge unfair laws.

Daily targets or lesson targets align to the same domain as the unit learning target. In other words, if the objective and learning target are in level four of Bloom's Revised Taxonomy, then the daily targets should also be level four. To break this down one more step so that students have bite-sized goals, see the following daily lesson targets:

- I can identify similarities in the approach Dr. Martin Luther King and Antigone both implemented.
- I can explain how nonviolent civil disobedience is used in "Letter from Birmingham Jail" and *Antigone.*
- I can recognize historical figures besides Dr. Martin Luther King and Antigone who have used nonviolent civil disobedience to challenge unfair laws.

Still with me? Remember that the objective is a level four. Because this objective came directly from the standard, which requires the student to "determine," we know students are required to conceptually process this component of the standard at a level four of Bloom's Revised Taxonomy in order to master it. This means the conceptual processes associated with the learning targets should align and therefore be at a level four.

Okay, so now guess what level of the Revised Bloom's Taxonomy (RBT) the assessment should be? You got it, level four.

Now let's look at the depth of the knowledge required by going back to Education 101 and reviewing Norman Webb's Degrees of Knowledge (DOK).

Webb's Degrees of Knowledge (DOK)

Norman Webb's Degrees of Knowledge (DOK) is a framework that organizes learning activities into four levels of rigor (Hess, 2004).

There are four levels:

1. Recollection and Reproduction or Recall. Does the student know the answer?
2. Knowledge Application. Students solve the problem or make decisions following correct methods.
3. Strategic Thinking. Students face abstract concepts and scenarios with more than one correct method.
4. Extended Critical Thinking. Students must creatively solve real-world problems with multiple sources of information, like a PBL, for example.

Like Bloom's Revised Taxonomy, there are specific verbs associated with each level of the framework in that helps educators determine the depth of the cognitive processes associated with the student's work.

In our example assignment on *Antigone* and ML King's "Letter from Birmingham Jail," (CCSS.ELA-Literacy.RL.9-10.2), students are asked to <u>analyze two pieces of literature</u>, which, as we discovered from deconstructing the standard, is a level four on Bloom's Revised Taxonomy.

What level is it on Webb's DOK? It is a level four DOK, or the highest level of rigor, using the Webb's Degrees of Knowledge framework.

Either using Bloom's Revised Taxonomy (BRT) or Webb's DOK, allows you to align your instruction and assessments with the standards and determine the level of engagement. Combined, you are able to determine the breadth (BRT) and depth (DOK) of the cognitive processes required of the student (Hess, 2004). The higher the level, the more rigorous or engaging the curriculum is, and you are more likely to *facilitate* instruction than be a sage on the stage. Remember the five traits of effective online curriculum? Does it surprise you that students are more interested in participating in thoughtful dialogue that compares their schoolwork to real-life than they are in completing vocabulary worksheets? Of course not, students are more successful in learner-centered environments.

Learner-centeredness, which is critical to a successful digital curriculum, occurs when instructional activities are "self-directed, authentic, and incorporate structured decision-making processes"(Rice, 2012, p.27). It is no coincidence that these three strategies are all in the higher levels of Bloom's Revised Taxonomy or in the higher levels of Webb's Degrees of Knowledge.

Now that your instructional activities are learner-centered and aligned, how do you determine the appropriate way(s) to assess your students? You definitely don't want to blow it on your assessment strategy after working so hard to align your instruction perfectly.

Selecting Appropriate Assessments

Think about the difference in authentic assessments and True/False tests. With an authentic assessment, there is a process of learning and work that takes place, not a specifically defined solution. Authentic assessments allow learning to look differently for each child. As mentioned previously, authentic assessments are learner-centered.

Allowing students to use technology to create a product is also ideal in the digital environment.

Incorporating the other traits for effective online curriculum into authentic assessments should not be difficult, as they naturally lend themselves to this instructional method. Create a space for reflection and one for collaboration in your digital course or workspace, and/or allow learners to define their own learning based on their interests and goals.

Let's revisit the learning target, for the breadth and depth of the learning target will drive the assessment method you use and ensure that your instruction and assessment strategies are aligned. In other words, I'm going to tell you how to guarantee you assess what you intend to measure. Of course, you will have to go back to your learning targets because they are essentially an outline for your assessment.

The first step is to categorize the learning target(s).

There are four categories or classifications:

- Knowledge or Factual Information about the topic (I describe, I define, I label)
- Reasoning or Procedural Knowledge (I demonstrate, I plan, I model)
- Higher Order Thinking (I compare, I contrast, I analyze)
- Product (I create a product)

Our learning target, "I can compare/contrast how Dr. Martin Luther King and Antigone use nonviolent civil disobedience to challenge unfair laws," requires higher order thinking. Using the explanations below, determine the type of target the assignment requires. Then, use the following chart from a 2012 Batelle for Kids training (Formative

Instructional Practices, n.d.) to determine the type of assessment to use to appropriately assess your learning target(s).

- Knowledge Targets—facts, procedures, conceptual understanding
- Reasoning Targets—solve problems, make inferences, draw conclusions, form judgements
- Skill Targets—demonstrating a physical skill
- Product Target—create a product

Learning Target	Selected Response	Written Response	Authentic Assessment	Personal Communication
Knowledge	*Good* Can assess targeted information and some relationships	*Strong* Can assess components of information and relationship among them	*Partial* Can assess elements of information and relationship among them in certain contexts	*Strong* Can assess elements of information
Reasoning	*Good* Can assess some patterns of reasoning	*Strong* Can assess all targets that require reasoning	*Partial* Can assess all targets that require reasoning specific to certain tasks and in certain contexts	*Strong* Can assess all reasoning targets
Skill	*Partial* Good match for measurement of skill targets only	*Poor* Cannot assess skill level; can only assess pre-requisite knowledge and reasoning	*Strong* Can observe and assess skills as they are being performed	*Partial* Strong match for some oral communication proficiencies

Product	*Poor* Can only assess prerequisite knowledge and reasoning	*Poor* Can only assess prerequisite knowledge and reasoning	Strong Can directly assess the attributes of quality products	Poor Can only assess prerequisite knowledge and reasoning

Now that you know the type of assessment, how many items of this type should you put on your overall assessment? Is there some requirement to always have 100 questions/items on a final exam?

In a word, "No."

The length of your assessment is truly a professional decision based on:

1) the purpose of the assessment

2) the type of learning target and assessment method

3) the characteristics of your students

With the exception of personal communication as a method for assessing your student, to determine the length of your assessment, you will have to determine the value of each learning target by importance. The easiest way to do this is to determine how much you emphasized the learning target in the instruction and curriculum that you developed.

If you spent 25% of the instructional time focusing on learning targets that should be assessed with selected response items, then 25% of your assessment should be made up of selected response. If 75% of the assessment is dedicated to a learning target, but you only spent 25% of your instructional time on it, then the assessment results will be misleading of student mastery and expectations (Chappuis, J., Stiggins, R., Chappuis, S., Arter, J. 2012; Rice, 2012; Sheninger & Murray, 2017). That would be like saying I want to want to be a master chef, so

I decide to compete in a national competition when I only cook about once a week. It just doesn't add up.

Types of Responses on Assessments

- Selected Response

Selected response items don't take long for students to complete, which means that if the topic is broad, you can include many selected response items to assess mastery of the learning target. Remember Mr. Smith, who taught social studies in high school? He had you read the chapter and answer the chapter questions as 100% of your instruction. Then he'd assign you a 100-item true/false test over the unit. Well, it turns out that although his class didn't include the traits of effective online courses, or effective face-to-face courses, for that matter; he did align his assessment to his instructional strategies. Selected response items are best for assessing individual pieces of knowledge.

Types of selected response include:

- Multiple choice
- True/False
- Matching
- Fill in the blank
- Written Response

When well done, written response items allow you to assess a student's knowledge *and* reasoning. They are applicable when assessing knowledge that interrelates or is related or with learning targets, where the learner is expected to reason (higher-order thinking). If you want to see what a student knows *and* how well the student understands it, then written response items are for you.

Students can compare/contrast, infer, analyze, and determine cause and effect with written response items. In what level of Bloom's or Webb's would you find those verbs? You betcha. They are at the top because they require critical thinking.

If you interrelate or interleave content, this also increases muscle memory, so there are even more reasons for written response. Since I mentioned muscle memory, for fun, notice how I asked you a question about the level of verb and made you think about something you read a while back? Spacing out memory retrieval causes your brain to create additional neural pathways. In layman's terms, I made you think harder to remember something you read a little earlier. This means you will be more likely to remember it. Try that on vocabulary quizzes for your kiddos (Brown, Roediger, McDaniel, 2014). Back to written response items.

Types of written response items include:

- Short answer (a sentence or two)
- Extended written response (several sentences to several paragraphs)

How do you know which of these two assessment types to use? Good question.

If the learning target requires the learner to demonstrate a conceptual understanding and the concept is not broad, then select short answer. If the learning target is more complex, then go with extended written response.

- Authentic Assessment

Does the learning target require the student to create a product? For example, if our learning target required students to create a letter in response to Dr. Martin Luther King, Jr., then the appropriate assessment type would be an authentic assessment because students are required to create a product. Whereas asking a student to list examples of civil disobedience within *Antigone* would be written response because the student is being asked to provide a list of reasons.

- Personal Communication

In the face-to-face classroom teachers gather a lot of information from students by asking instructional questions. Believe it or not, this is an assessment strategy.

Ways in which online instructors can ask instructional questions online include:

- Teacher-to-learner interaction
- Teacher-to-class during live lessons
- Discussion boards
- Conferences during office hours
- Online journals or portfolios
- Oral exams (think webinar, FaceTime, phone)

Selecting a sample size for assessments through personal communication is a little different than the other assessment types. Mainly, you need to decide whether you are able to gather enough evidence to support the learning target and whether you are able to gather enough information from the student to determine if he or she mastered the learning target. Often times, personal communications are used more in formative assessments for learning rather than summative assessments of learning. Make sure you give students the appropriate wait time when using this strategy, and if you are interested in the assessment of learning (summative), make sure to use this strategy one-on-one with students during your office hours (Chappuis, J., Stiggins, R., Chappuis, S., Arter, J. 2012; Rice, 2012; Sheninger & Murray, 2017). This assessment style is a great way to also be certain that the individual student is submitting authentic work.

So, what type of assessment would you select for our learning target? If you said, extended written response, which in this case is an authentic assessment, then you are definitely ready to create the backbone of your online class.

Whew! That was fun. Wasn't it?

Remember, the process we just went through is the first step in developing or designing your own digital resources after you know the model your school or program will be using for digital instruction. In the design phase of your digital resources, as you create your alignment, you will decide on the objectives, learning targets, and assessments that will teach and measure the standards you are required to teach. Like an architect building a house, you now have the blueprint information for your online course. This is the first step in designing an effective online course. At the core, this work is no different than designing effective curriculum for the traditional classroom. Consistency or alignment in identifying the appropriate required level and depth of cognitive processes is critical for student learning.

If you work this hard to create a good assessment, let's make sure you communicate effectively about it with your students. Let's talk rubrics.

RUBRICS

It may or may not seem strange that I'm including an entire section on rubrics. But I have yet to review an online course or a blended course that has a good rubric in it. I'm not wearing an almighty assessment hat when I say this. The reason for my concern is that students in an online class do not always have a face-to-face opportunity to ask clarifying questions around assignments. So, the expectations they know of are either in the instructions or in the rubric.

That being said, when I see very vague rubrics that simply indicate whether the work is done or not, I see no guidance or communication to the student which is the point of the rubric. This is a tremendous area of needed improvement for digital education. And it's an area, that with intent and thoughtful planning, will certainly help students improve their work toward meeting teacher expectations.

Task Rubric

A rubric that is specific to a task (task rubric) usually isn't handed out before an assignment, but there are cases where this might be appropriate. If you are assessing a specific learning target, you would use a task rubric as opposed to a general rubric, which can be generalized across tasks.

Examples:

TASK RUBRIC FOR DRESSING FOR COLD WEATHER

4 points: Dressed appropriately (includes 2 gloves, hat)

3 points: Dressed with 2 gloves, 0 hat

2 points: Dressed with 1 glove, 0 hat

1 point: Dressed with 0 gloves, 0 hat

0 points: Not dressed, 0 hat, 0 gloves

GENERAL RUBRIC FOR A LITERATURE ASSIGNMENT

4 points: Interprets information from literature to provide correct answers. Provides accurate and complete descriptive details.

3 points: Interprets information from literature. Provides some accurate and complete descriptive details.

2 points: Interprets some information from literature. Does not provide accurate or complete descriptive details.

1 point: Interprets little information from literature. Does not provide accurate or complete descriptive details.

0 points: Does not interpret information from literature. Does not provide accurate or complete descriptive details.

To create a task specific rubric, refer to the learning target you are assessing. From there, create a sentence that represents a conceptual understanding.

Then list what the following three types of understanding look like in context to the assessment:

- Partial understanding
- Misunderstanding
- Lack of understanding

Now you have your rubric levels. Let's practice with a short answer three-point rubric, "Shakespeare's play, *Romeo and Juliet* is a tragedy, although most people think it is a Romance play" as the proposition.

ASSESSMENT ITEM:

Is *Romeo and Juliet* a tragedy or a romance play? Why?

SCORING GUIDE:

2 Points: *Romeo and Juliet* is a tragedy because the two young lovers commit suicide to be together as a result of their feuding families. (complete understanding)

1 Point: *Romeo and Juliet* is both a tragedy and a romance. The play ends with the death of two lovers, but the entire play is about them falling in love. (partial understanding)

0 Point: *Romeo and Juliet* is a romance because Romeo and Juliet fall in love. (lack of, partial or misunderstanding, major flaw=no point)

If I wanted to add a task rubric for a lengthier assessment item, something besides short answer or extended response, I'd make it a four-point rubric. I'd do this by adding an item between 0 and 1 on the current scoring guide (above), where I'd give the point only if there was no critical flaw in the response.

In other words, in the three-point rubric, a fatal flaw in the response automatically means the student gets zero points. However, in a four-point rubric, lack of partial or misunderstanding would be separated out from a response with a major flaw and would receive a higher point of one.

General rubrics can be used with and apply to any task, so they are easier to make than task specific. Plus, they can be repurposed (Chappuis et al., 2012; Rice, 2012; Sheninger & Murray, 2017).

2 Points
Complete understanding

1 Point
Partial understanding, no misunderstandings

0 Points
Lack of understanding, complete misunderstanding, partial with a "major flaw"

Now that you have completed the planning of your course backbone by:

1. deconstructing your standards,
2. creating your objectives, and
3. your learning targets…

How do you bring this stuff to life for students in a digital environment? Let's move onto actually creating and curating content.

CHAPTER 6

TO CREATE OR CURATE?

DESIGN GUIDELINES

I will forewarn you that the technical design of digital content is much more difficult than curating online resources. What is the difference? Curating resources is when you pull together resources that already exist. You then organize these resources in order to teach your learning targets.

Actually, designing digital curriculum from scratch, is a completely different undertaking. First, I will remind you, as we discussed in Chapter 5, that there are designers who specialize in this. If you are focused on teaching, then you do not necessarily have time to develop an online class from scratch. You may have to, depending on your situation, but your primary focus should be the students. Within this focus you have a priority to curate resources that are high quality, align to your learning targets, and meet the interests and needs of your learners. I don't know too many teachers who have time to truly develop online content from scratch while managing all the other priorities of teaching online. I'm going to share some design guidelines that I generally follow when leading teams who create digital curriculum. These are also guidelines I apply when evaluating resources that I curate for instruction.

At the core, good instruction is good instruction (Is this in your brain yet? Good!). It is essential to pique the curiosity of the learner. Regardless of medium, educators are taught to open a lesson with a hook in order to gain the learner's attention. We also know that people learn from stories or narratives. We always have, be it oral, written, digital…or something else. We know that people are more willing to learn when they are happy. Endorphins are released when you laugh, causing information being learned to transfer to long-term memory. We know that pictures of primal instincts and people with faces and emotions draw the attention of our brains. These foundational learning elements do not change regardless of whether learning is taking place online or in person. What does change is the way in which learners *interact* with new knowledge.

Let's begin by examining the look and feel of digital resources. The design should "stay out of the way." If the design of the resource is distracting to the learner, then it completely defeats the purpose because it gets in the way of the learning and processing of the material. Did you know that overusing colors and other visual elements has been shown to decrease learning outcomes? Remember when you first learned PowerPoint? Did you use every transition and every animation known to man? I won't tell if you won't.

In short, less is more. You want to select a resource that reduces the overall cognitive load. What do I mean by this? You want the learner to think about the content, not about the crazy website or PowerPoint. Simply put, the less brain power that is taken to interpret the background or layout, the more brainpower that can be used to focus on learning.

If you ever sponsored the school yearbook or the school newspaper (oh yeah—I did), then your skills will definitely come into use. When you develop or review resources make sure they are visually appealing with margins and functional areas. A simple rule? No flashy or trashy, please. Look for balance. Make sure that the layouts you choose (even in your PowerPoints, Google Slides, or Prezis) create meaning. Make the most important content dominant with size and placement. We naturally think things at the top and on the left are more important.

Aesthetics matter. You may find the greatest resource ever published on your learning target, but if it is outdated with terrible graphics, I suggest you go with your second favorite, if the graphics are better. Students perform better when the interface is more attractive. This is because emotions impact learning. In our brains aesthetics equals usability. We perform better when we have a more appealing design from which to learn. What also may be of interest to you is the Mayer's Multimedia Principle, which states that images combined with words are remembered better than just text alone, as long as the graphics are relevant.

Additionally, when you are curating resources, make sure you select those that use appropriate signifiers so that learners can focus on learning rather than operating the interface. In other words, make sure buttons look clickable. If something is underlined, then make sure it links to something. You don't want your learners spending time trying to figure out how to navigate; you want them learning the content.

Specifically, when you create content, you want about 100 characters to a line, ideally 45-72 (think tweets). Don't center or right align text, and definitely don't put the instructions in a decorative font. Believe it or not, *learners think the task is harder than it really is* when the instructions are presented this way. Our brains interpret importance based on shading. **The bolder something is the more important it is**. The more pastel it is, the less important it is.

Remember that you don't want your digital resources to simply be an e-textbook. When curating or designing resources, you will want learners to interact with the content frequently. Interaction can be answering questions, clicking a button, or any other way in which the learner can demonstrate control of his or her learning, besides, of course scrolling through pages. This strategy combined with the actual design of the content will allow for active learning and participation.

Your greatest area of concern when designing or curating resources is accessibility. I could write an entire book on designing and reviewing resources to meet accessibility guidelines. Please refer to Exceptional Education section of this chapter for more information on accessibility. If you have further interest check out the W3C accessibility guidelines online at www.w3.org.

FINDING THE RESOURCES

Now you know what to look for as far as alignment, and you have a solid expectation when it comes to design. Where do you go to find decent resources? Since you are an educator, everything falls under Fair Use, right? Uhhhmmmm.... No. This is where you need to pay close attention to website "terms of use" and "privacy policies." This isn't exactly exciting stuff, but you really should read before you check the box and agree to the terms every app or website you go to.

STUDENT PRIVACY

Let's review why passwords and user identifications, among other methods for data protection, are so important. We have a regulation in the United States to protect student privacy called Family Education

Rights and Privacy Act (FERPA). I'm sure you have heard a lot about protecting sensitive data online for yourself, and you may have your own concerns about your students' data being available online. As a result, I'm going to go into a bit of detail, so you will be informed and can make sure when you select resources you choose content from providers where students' sensitive information is being protected. This is extremely important, not only at school but also at home.

Under the "Protection of Pupil Rights Amendment," (PPRA) parents have the right to opt out of any activity that would expose any "Personally Identifiable Information" (PII) for their child. Personally Identifiable Information contains direct identifiers such as family members' names or student names and indirect identifiers such as date of birth, place of birth or mother's maiden name. So, under PPRA, if a child is taking a digital course that requires PII, then a parent can request that the child be given the course in paper format instead. This would obviously be because the parent is concerned that PII would be accessed by the wrong person or organization online. In context, an example of this may be that a parent is afraid an estranged, abusive parent could discover the whereabouts of his child by tracking him down online. Or perhaps a parent is afraid a child's social security number would be stolen by a thief. These are, of course, extreme examples, but I use them to illustrate the point. Given this, before you require a student to use any resources, you have an obligation to review the privacy policies and the terms of use.

You also should be aware that under FERPA the school has the right to release directory information, which is information such as students' names, addresses, telephone listings, emails, dates and/or places of birth, pictures, weights and heights of athletes, degrees, and awards. This is why identifiable information is listed in yearbooks and athletic or music programs. However, under PPRA, since this is PII, a parent, has the right to opt out by requesting that the school not include or identify her child, if there is a concern. This doesn't come up too frequently in online learning because most educators use Software as a Services (SaaS), or software that the school district has paid a licensing fee to use. This means the district has a signed contract in place to protect student data.

All of this is extremely important information to know, though, especially when you, as a teacher, begin to curate resources in the digital environment. Let me give you an example. I'm sure you heard of, if not used or have recommended Khan Academy, an online or digital provider of curriculum. Many schools use their math content, for example. They have been featured on 20/20, Nightline...you name it, but an investigation by *EdWeek*, and an educational journal, in 2014 found that they "are essentially enabling third parties to gather unlimited information about users and disclaiming any responsibility" (Edsurge, 2014). This is a bit alarming since parental permission isn't requested. This data is old, but I share this example because Khan is reputable, and I suspect that if you review their privacy policy today you will find that it is lengthy and challenging to read. Additionally, I suspect you will find that 3rd party data is released on some levels still. Chapter 11 includes more information on data collection to include highlights of privacy laws for households in California and online users in the European Union.

Generally, anything ending in .gov is a good resource and does not collect user data. With the exception of government sites, free is never free. Usually, if a resource is free, then user data is being compromised. It is your responsibility to read the terms of use and the privacy policy of the provider for whom you are curating resources for your students. Additionally, students should not be asked to sign up for user accounts and passwords without parental permission, unless they are over the age of 18. There are some great resources that you will find but may have to ask parents to set up user accounts for their children. Please do not ask children to set up their own accounts, even if it is much more convenient.

FAIR USE

Speaking of free, as tempting as it may be, someone else's work is not your own to use freely. Fair Use does not mean that you can copy someone else's work or use it freely since you are in education. We should always model best practices for our students. How hard is it to, at the least, add a link to where you found the information you may want to include in what you are designing? I know, this is one more step, and you are already overworked. However, as educators, we have to model academic integrity for our students. I'm all about shopping and getting ideas from resources, but straight out copying, now that just isn't cool. So, if you aren't copying, then what is it called when you use someone else's resources? After all, you aren't writing a research paper, and if you had time to create the resources yourself, you would. Welcome to the world of curating resources.

CURATING

Obviously, when you curate digital resources, you want to find the best ones available to teach your specific objectives or learning targets. This begins with recognizing the quality of the digital resource. Like I have said multiple times, and you have read in previous chapters "Good instruction is good instruction." For this reason, again, we will revisit Education 101 as I walk you through the process of selecting and bringing digital content to life.

At the core of good lesson design, is good learning theory. Some of these theories include: Constructivist, Directed Instruction, Cognitivism, Brain-based, Behaviorism…, and some learning theories do lend themselves better to the online environment.

If you are an objectivist, don't put the book down so fast. Hang in here with me for a few more paragraphs. There is absolutely a role for direct instruction/teacher-led activities and constructivist models in digital education. In digital education, the technology associated with the learning is what allows for both learning theories to co-exist in order to personalize learning for the student. Using both theories truly creates a better learning experience for students. For example, you may have a Response To Intervention (RTI) tool that is adaptive based on a student's performance. Who would turn that down? A student would immediately be provided access to content at the exact level he or she needs without you lifting a finger. That is better than a gift card to Target!

Meanwhile, your mainstream curriculum uses whole group instruction and meets the requirements of 1-5 above. With this model, you have the best of both worlds.

You are able to teach the whole group while personalizing and meeting the needs of individual students without:

- individual students knowing that each is getting a different level of content, and
- without lifting a finger.

Based on this model, you don't have to create individualized assessments or individualized benchmarks for every child in order to offer a personalized directed instruction component of your instructional model because you have software to do this for you. This enables you to identify and analyze data associated with the directed instruction of the RTI tool for individual tutoring sessions with students which further enables you to engage your students and build rapport. Further, you have more opportunities for students, during your engaging self-developed and/or licensed content, to engage higher-order-thinking skills. In short, it makes you a better teacher while saving you time and effort.

Another way to teach using both objective and constructivist teaching philosophies is by customizing curriculum based on pre-assessment scores. Again, this is much easier in the digital environment because the technology does a lot of, if not all, of the work for you. Based on pre-test scores, if students show mastery of specific skills, then certain units are not be visible to them. The visible units can be designed using constructivist learning theories, which tend to meet the five requirements outlined by Rice (2012) in a previous chapter more often than objective classrooms. In this curriculum model, students would benefit from the best of both worlds, and just as described in the previous paragraph, you are freed up to facilitate and develop a rapport with the children.

LEARNER AUTONOMY IN CURRICULUM DESIGN

Research tells us that there are ways in which to design curriculum that is more conducive to student learning. John Hattie's (2009) meta-analysis of over 800 studies ranked influences that impact student learning outcomes or student achievement. His research continued, and in 2015, he released a 1200 study meta-analysis. He found that the key to making a difference in student learning is making learning visible, which he describes in his 2011 book, *Visible Learning for Teachers*. What Hattie consistently discovered is that student achievement is impacted by the same variables. Further, he investigated effect size (Cohen's d) to see which factors impact student achievement the most. Within this statistical analysis that reports the effect size of an intervention, Cohen's d, 0.2 is considered a small effect size, .5 is a medium effect size, and .8 is a large effect size. The closer the effect size gets to 1.0, the greater the impact the variable has. Hattie ranked the effect sizes of 150 variables in 2011 in *Visible Learning for Teachers*. Self-reported grades scored 1.44.

This score is much higher than other variables, so since self-reported grades had an effect score of +1.44, you might want to consider including similar strategies in your courses or curated resources by having students set goals, self-assess, or, in other words, self-regulate. "Online learning environments provide a unique opportunity for teachers to use the various features to cultivate student self-regulation" (Lock et al., 2017, p.1). When students self-regulate, whether they are in a face-to-face class or an online class, they are more successful.

In the online classroom students have flexibility and autonomy by the very nature of the model. If the curriculum is designed in such a way to encourage self-monitoring and student choice, then your instructional strategies can really take advantage of the online environment. You do this quite simply by:

- Ask students to set goals at the beginning of the class (academic, pacing).
- Give students choices for assignments. Allow them ownership in the final task.
- Provide multiple checkpoints or knowledge checks for students to self-assess.
- Offer benchmarks.
- Set up discussion boards where students interact and reflect on learning experiences.
- Ask students to collaborate with peers.

- If the Learning Management System (LMS) allows, ask students to reflect on longitudinal performance data.
- If the LMS includes a digital backpack, list study habits, learning preferences, hobbies, etc....

It is essential that while you are offering the student the opportunity to self-direct, you also keep in mind the Dunning-Kruger affect, which is when people naturally over-estimate their own abilities. For this reason, you need to have multiple opportunities for students to self-assess and to get regular feedback from you, the instructor. This helps learners to recognize their true skillset rather than judging based on their own self-perception. For example, the reason students may study flashcards of new vocabulary words only 2-3 times and feel confident they know the knowledge, is because they are over-confident.

In your course, you should regularly require students to self-assess so that they actually see a reflection of the information they know. This will also provide you feedback on which knowledge or content area(s) is mastered. Additionally, each time you assess, keep spacing out the assessment or retrieval of knowledge that has been previous studied (Brown et al., 2014). This will aid in learning by repeating previously taught information, increasing synapses, and by causing retrieval as you scaffold.

DESIGN ACTIVE PARTICIPATION FOR STUDENTS

In order to design a digital classroom where students will be actively engaged or participating, your design must be intentional, much like when you design content to be engaging in a typical classroom. Just like in the traditional classroom, when students are actively engaged, your classroom management problems are usually solved. When we think of active participation in a traditional classroom, we envision children in cooperative learning groups; racing to complete games; or working in teams to meet a common goal; but what does this look like in the online classroom?

Actually, the online classroom creates the ideal lens for active participation because you can filter for the judgment that takes place in the traditional classroom by removing the assumptions or anxieties that come with face-to-face instruction. This allows students to be free to focus on the content and not on their appearances or other areas in which they may be self-conscious such as their ability to read aloud, for example.

A student I had the opportunity to work with years ago, who was a second language learner and deaf in one ear, was much more confident in an online class than in a traditional classroom. In the traditional classroom, sometimes she didn't hear the teacher clearly, and she was embarrassed to ask questions because of her language barrier. In the online classroom, she could look up words in the classroom instructions or content with which she wasn't familiar, or she could reread them. Also, she wasn't embarrassed to read aloud. No other students knew if she reached out to her teacher to ask questions. She was overjoyed with online learning because it was a great fit for her. More recently a friend of mine taught an EL student, who scored higher than all other students in her online English course. The online model created an opportunity for him to reread materials and speak without worry about what his classmates thought.

As we discussed in Chapter 4, students are engaged when they are working in areas of higher-order thinking. What is the purpose of an online course where students complete worksheets or only answer matching or level 1 DOK questions?

As you design and curate your resources, make sure to align your learning targets (for clarification see Chapter 5). Don't select a learning object simply because it is based on the same topic as your lesson. Your students definitely won't be engaged if they are reading an e-textbook and simply answering chapter questions for eighteen weeks. A textbook can deliver this. In order to design a course with active participation you have to be intentional with your strategies. You want the content you design or select to align and scaffold appropriately, and you also want to deliver instruction that encourages:

- Learner autonomy
- Active participation
- Collaboration and community building
- Authentic assessment
- Acquisition of 21st century skills (Rice, 2012, p. 27)

Building a blended or online course marries rich content with strong pedagogy. This is what separates it from an e-textbook or a distance learning course, and, ultimately, this is what encourages students to be actively engaged.

LIVE LESSONS

When designing active participation for students, you cannot overlook the benefit of live lessons. Not only do they offer an opportunity for learner:learner and learner:instructor interaction, but these types of interactions create a great opportunity for you to include SEL strategies in your class. These interactions go beyond 1:1 tutoring sessions or meetings during office hours.

Exactly, what are live lessons, and how do you design them effectively? There is no one size fits all. I have found that all teachers do them a little differently, and you have to decide what fits best for your style and the requirements of your program. Since the majority of online curriculum is asynchronous, where students work independently and at their own pace, or if they are required to meet specific timelines, students can work when it is convenient for them or their family, with the exception of assessments. For this reason, students do not log in to a live classroom, for the most part, unless the model is a 100% synchronous experience. In other words, for the most part, students are not expected to log into their digital classes for one-on-one instruction or classroom instruction at a specific time during the day with their instructors. Because of this, teachers sometimes find it difficult to require and hold students accountable for live lessons in their online classes.

There are some programs, though, such as Stanford Online High School, which target advanced students, that do require/offer synchronous or online instruction. This model increases instructor:student and student:student interactions. During the Covid19 pandemic, some school models offered live instruction, and some required synchronous instruction for the families who elected for remote instruction. Models ranged from live instruction for a set period of time each day or week to fully synchronous or live models. My daughter's school, for example, required students who opted for remote learning to log in synchronously for the entire school day. For her school, and for her as a learner, the model worked great!

During regular circumstances, though, most online programs, are designed for students to work at a flexible pace and location with minimal live or real-time interaction with the instructor. Of the real-time interaction that is required, the live instruction can be done during a teacher's office hours, where the online instructor is directly accessible to the students for a limited period of time. A teacher may reach out directly to a student for one-on-one tutoring or vice versa. Another common alternative for synchronous instruction is often called a "Live Lesson." Some teachers use this time for extra tutoring or to teach a lesson related to the content to a group of students at one time.

There have been mixed feelings regarding live lessons in traditionally asynchronous programs over the years. So, don't be too hard on yourself if you don't feel successful during your first live lesson.

If you are an experienced online teacher, unless your program requires live lessons, it is possible that you haven't implemented these. Some programs and experienced online teachers feel as though they spend significant time preparing for live lessons, yet students do not take them seriously because the live lessons forego the flexibility students expected when they signed up for the program, they may be unable to attend. Still yet, when students do attend, they may do so out of resentment and not out of good faith or academic fortitude. For these reasons, some teachers feel frustration and doubt the value of the live lessons. On the other hand, other teachers have no doubt there is value in live lessons because they have seen the value students gain from attending the lessons, and they have observed connections students make to the curriculum based on their higher levels of interaction and their clarified understandings of the content. Herein lies the conundrum. To include live lessons or not to include live lessons?

If it is good for kids why wouldn't you do it? There are ways to work smarter when it comes to live lessons and not bury yourself in more work, and there are ways to engage students in the live lessons. In theory, live lessons make sense, even if a student attends a recorded session, if, say he or she has a scheduling conflict. Including live lessons builds rapport between instructors and students. Live lessons create a community of learners, especially when the live lessons connect the content to the real world.

Let's dive into that last one a bit. My suggestion is to make your live lessons connect the content to higher-order thinking and relate it to something students see in the real world. How can you do this? Take a current event that relates to your content area, regardless of grade level, and make it applicable. This prevents you from teaching eight different live lessons in one day.

Sample Live Lesson:

I taught secondary English online and face-to-face. For kicks and giggles, I just went to NPR and pulled the first current event article under Health as a challenge to see if I could work whatever came up into a Live Lesson by relating it to my content area; thereby relating to the real world. To access the article either go to the following address or scan the QR code.

www.npr.org/sections/goatsandsoda/2020/08/28/907106441/
coronavirus-faq-is-it-safe-to-get-on-the-bus-or-subway

The news article I found, "Coronavirus: Is it safe to get on the bus or subway?" was a discussion on whether it is safe to travel using public transportation during the Covid19 Pandemic (August 29, 2020).

For a Live Lesson I:

- Read the article together with the students.
- Put the students in break-out groups in Zoom and ask them to discuss the article and be able to answer a series of questions, ultimately ending in, "Would you ride a use public transportation if you had a family to support and were an essential worker with no other means of transportation? What are the risks? Why would you choose to do this or not choose to do this?"
- Each group would create a Venn Diagram to organize their thoughts comparing the benefits and the risks of riding a bus during a pandemic.
- I would bring the groups back together and have the reporter from each group share each group's findings.
- From there we would discuss via a PowerPoint the article is an example of "Man v. Societal Pressure or Man v. Nature."
- Students would be required to submit a Venn Diagram as a compare contrast comparing the conflict as Societal Pressure and/or Nature for an essential worker during the pandemic who must provide for a family while having to rely on public transportation.
- Depending on the age group of the students, there may be a required writing assignment as the next step of the reflection required.

During your live lesson, make an effort not to lecture. Remember the goal is to have the learners do the work. You do not want to be the sage on the stage. You want the lessons to be an opportunity for the students to interact and participate in the learning. Present the students with a topic and put them in breakout rooms to collaborate and think critically how to solve problems that relate to community or career. Make sure they have specific tasks with rubrics to guide them on your expectations. Then bring them back together for presentations or resolutions.

Problem and/or project-based learning are ideal in the online environment and live lessons. My example is not a problem or project-based lesson, but how interesting would it be to take my live lesson idea to the next step? Ask students to come up with a solution for someone in this situation. If you are an essential worker, have a family to feed, and have no transportation of your own, what are ways to reduce your risk of infection without relying on public transportation? If they deem that the conflict is Man v. Societal Pressure, how could they solve the problem?

Elementary teachers, imagine what fun you could have problem solving with three-dimensional objects, for example. Math teachers, live lessons could be used to bring to live the formulas students are studying. I've seen pigs dissected, where each child has a pig, and the class dissects his pig via camera along with the teacher in a live lesson. It was probably the neatest live lesson I've ever seen!

While many online students flourish from the social interaction, others may be nervous, but the psychological distance of being online rather than in person does allow for more confidence. Additionally, you may consider providing students with reading materials, podcasts, or videos ahead of the live lesson so that they can feel more prepared. For example, with my example lesson, it would have been helpful to English language learners or students who are not as confident with their reading if I had sent out the link to the article in advance of the live lesson. Then they would have had time to read in advance of the lesson rather than being on the spot and reading with the group.

One of the benefits of online learning is that students have time to compose their thoughts or ideas before responding in discussion forums. Although "live," there are ways to increase student confidence online just by helping them be prepared.

"To grade or not to grade" a live lesson? Ugh. This question is not so easy. In truth, it depends on the model and requirements of your program. If students are required to attend live lessons, then obviously, you have to follow required procedures. But what if you are simply trying to encourage collaboration and critical thinking while maintaining the flexibility of the online model? Some programs require students to attend a specific number of live lessons monthly, while others do not require any at all. If your program doesn't require attendance to live lessons, but you want to encourage learner-to-learner interaction, you could offer extra credit for attending and participating. Remember that families all have different schedules and connectivity challenges, so I suggest that you offer a morning, afternoon, and evening session. It would be even better to survey your students and determine times that would be convenient for them.

Don't forget that when you offer live lessons, parents are participating/ watching often times. This is a lot like having an observer in your classroom. Parents are curious about how online learning works. Once they see a few live lessons they are no longer interested because they see that their children are actually participating and learning. Also, remember that you will be "entering" homes of students, so it is best to set some ground rules and expectations. Train students to mute unless talking. For example, should you suggest that students be in school uniform or require that they be dressed? This and timeliness are *not* unreasonable. Let's not forget that students may wander around their homes with their devices during live lessons if they aren't observing the best practice of having a set workstation. In that case, it is a good idea to make sure parents are aware of the time you offer live lessons. You wouldn't want siblings or family members wandering past the camera in various states of dress or dancing in the background.

A few takeaway notes on Live Lessons:

- Communication expectations in advance of live lesson
    - Microphone on mute unless called on
    - Raise hand
    - Dressed appropriately
    - Cameras on
    - Turn students "off" if they don't follow expectations
- Communicate grading requirements in advance of live lesson
- Create engaging lessons by relating to the real-world and their lives
- Manage your time wisely
    - Set up breakout groups in advance
    - Have sites and presentations queued and ready
- Be familiar with your video tool in advance
- Show video clips or have students read current events
- Have students do the work
- Use project or problem-based learning to engage learners
- Use the time to develop a rapport with students
- Encourage learner-learner interaction

Remember, even if the content you have (or the content you don't have) doesn't include an assignment you want students to do, there is nothing wrong with a good ole' fashioned Word document with instructions that students receive via email. Don't let perfect be the enemy of good. You can absolutely supplement any content with your ideas unless, of course, your program doesn't allow for this. Let's say, though, you are teaching blended, but you have a fabulous traditional, face-to-face assignment that has worked for years. There is no definition that says you cannot implement it in addition to what you are doing that is digital. Blended is a mixture of all things great. If you are teaching online, and you want to work in your fabulous traditional assignment, have your students join on Zoom or Google Meet. Don't throw out the baby with the bathwater. At the end of the day, this is about kids and helping them learn based on the way their brains and our society is shifting as a result of technology. We have to remember, though, that good instruction is and always will be good instruction. Has that sunk in yet?

EXCEPTIONAL EDUCATION

Obviously, not all students will possess the traditional characteristics of successful online learners, so you will need to continually analyze data to engage your students. Interestingly, digital education can be the ideal learning environment for students with exceptional needs depending on their particular challenge. I've seen many students flourish online that were very unsuccessful in the traditional classroom. I have also seen schools and parents try to force online learning on students where it isn't a good fit. It is essential to evaluate an exceptional education student to determine if online learning is a good fit prior to enrolling the student in an online class.

Regardless of exceptionality status, successful online students typically share common traits (Rice, 2012). They:

- Have competent computer skills
- Have time to devote to class
- Are organized
- Have good written and communication skills
- Take responsibility for their own learning
- Have confidence in their abilities
- Have a high level of motivation
- Have additional adult support

If you have a student in your blended or online classroom, don't be afraid to reach out for support from the school or district. It is critical you know the modifications and accommodations required to meet the child's need, as they are listed in the student's Individual Education Plan (IEP), to determine if the required modifications and accommodations can be met in your online course. These modifications and accommodations are required by law, so you want to make sure you are able to support students in the way they need to be successful, while abiding by the laws. Just like in the traditional classroom, you can expect approximately 15% of your students to have IEPs.

Once you know the modification(s)/accommodation(s) for a child, you need to determine if the digital content you have allows for the modification(s). If you have prescribed content, find out if the design follows Universal Design for Learning (UDL). If the content provider follows the guidelines set by UDL, then the curriculum will be much easier for a student with disabilities to access. UDL was deliberately created for students with disabilities. Learning material is presented in multiple ways within the content, for example. Another feature to check for is text-to-speech. Does the content or electronic tools you are using have a read aloud function (text-to-speech)? This feature helps with English Language Learners, students who are behind grade-level literacy, students with specific learning disability (SLD), or students with vision challenges. Remember, too, that just because the content claims to have text-to-speech, this doesn't mean it will be understandable. If possible, actually listen to the content yourself to make sure it is understandable. Be familiar with your contacts in case any of your students need adaptive equipment for their keyboards or the mouse. A critical resource that may be useful to you is a document called a VPAT. This document is provided by vendors, and it will list all the accommodations the software offers. Above and beyond what is listed in the VPAT, it may be necessary for you or your school/district to be creative in order to meet the needs of a particular student.

Typically, the following modifications are seen for online students:

- Extended time on tests
- Additional submissions (more attempts) on assignments
- .pdf documents or notes delivered ahead of time
- Screen reader or text-to-speech
- Response to intervention (RTI)
- Placement in the course based on the results of a diagnostic pretest

Since you are pulling from the same pool of students online that you are for traditional instruction, for the most part, you won't have different modifications or see different disabilities than you would for students in the traditional classroom. However, you may see that some students tend to perform better in the online classroom. For example, I have seen that a handful of students with Autism perform better in the online classroom. I cannot scientifically speak to why this is because the sample size with which I have observed this over the years has not been large enough. What I can tell you is that parents of children with Autism have all been incredibly grateful for the experience with digital curriculum in the programs I have overseen. Autism manifests itself differently with each child, but each parent suggested the lack of distraction for one reason or another as the cause for success (less classroom distraction, less noise, fewer concepts on which to focus at one time…) in each situation I experienced with a child with Autism online. Please keep in mind, though, these were very structured environments with very specific curriculum guidelines. You may find you need to alter or add to these suggestions when teaching individuals with Autism in a pandemic environment.

Let's dig into some law. Remember the Individuals with Disabilities Education Act (IDEA)? It does apply to digital education, sort of. If you are in a district and implementing blended learning, if you are teaching online for a district, or if you are working for an online provider to offer part-time supplemental courses through the school or school district, then the school or district is responsible for IDEA because the student "belongs" to the school. This includes determining whether the student has special needs, developing the IEP if appropriate, and putting the student in the least restrictive environment (LRE) if an IEP is required. Many times, the bulk of what I just mentioned falls on the School Psychologist or Special Education department. However, no matter the student's ability or status, if you suspect something, remember documentation of data is your best friend. The more documentation you have on progress, or lack thereof, including any work you suggested for RTI, the better equipped you and your school will be to support and provide what these amazing students need for successful online learning.

The Americans with Disabilities Act (ADA) applies to digital education regarding facilities and equitable access. If you are teaching in a school building, then the facilities should already be compliant, but if you are using a computer lab, and for some reason a disabled student cannot access the equipment needed in the lab, then you would be out of compliance. I have encouraged parents who have students with Individual Education Plans (IEP) that need digital courses to have this need documented in the child's plans so that associated fees would be covered by the district. Since ADA includes equitable access and is part of the Civil Rights Act we may see growth in opportunity for students with 504 plans to take digital courses in the future.

If you are considering teaching for a full-time online school I would ask if they have a special needs policy outlining the responsibilities of everyone involved. For example, will you be expected to attend IEP meetings? How are services such as speech therapy provided to students whose IEP requires such services? Is there someone on staff that specializes in special education?

When designing your own curriculum for blended or online learning, keep the needs of exceptional education students in mind. A small step to start with is labeling all images in your presentations with alt tags. If a student is visually impaired and is using a screen reader, labeling the image with an alt tag will allow the screen reader to tell the child what the image is. Some other quick tips include:

- Make sure you present content in small chunks,
- Allow students to submit assignments to you through various formats: written, verbal, video....
- Provide students with an outline of the important take-aways of a passage rather than having them read the entire document.

- Give students a graphic organizer to complete during any lecture.
- Give students with special needs such as ADD or ADHD special jobs during blended sessions or live lessons.
- Set up a time for parents to pick up manipulatives or other tactile supports that are required by the IEP.
- Provide 1:1 support in a "breakout room" with peer-tutoring, or a parent volunteer.

The critical component of having students with exceptional needs in your digital class is understanding the modifications and accommodations within the child's IEP, implementing the modifications and accommodations, communicating with the child and the family, and documenting any and all implementation trials as well as the child's responses to those modifications. You will find that some children with exceptional needs soar in the digital environment and seeing their confidence skyrocket is absolutely rewarding. Other students will struggle, but in the end, they and their families will have had a solid learning experience that will, hopefully, help them to grow through their educational challenges.

While a tremendous amount of planning and design goes into a solid digital curriculum, once the foundation is laid, modifying and improving the curated or designed resources is not nearly as time consuming. It is critical, though, to be in the mindset of students when you design or curate learning activities. Students obviously would find no interest in the same topics that Boomers would, for example. What do we know about our current students and how can we get inside their heads to understand their motivation and perspectives so that any content we curate or design is actually of interest to them?

CHAPTER 7

KNOWING YOUR STUDENTS (AND THEIR BRAINS)

If you cannot write code or implement fancy games, how will you keep students coming back for more? After all, you need them to be willing and interested in logging in on a daily basis, not to mention completing assignments regularly, in order for them to be successful. We know most K-12 students are not independent or auditory learners, and you aren't reading this because you want to design a correspondence course like old school distance learning. Let's examine this generation a bit more to see what makes it tick since this is a generation raised on edutainment. Much like distance learning, you cannot rely on your physical presence, your charming good looks, or your engaging personality like you can in the face-to-face classroom to keep students engaged in an online class.

Here are some amazing statistics about youngsters and their exposure to technology as edutainment.

- 90% of parents with children under 2 let their kids use electronic media (Braiker, 2013).

- In 2011, 52% of homes with children ages 8 and younger had access to a mobile device.
- In 2015, 24% of kids ages 8-12 had their own smartphone. In just four years, that number increased to 41% (Rideout & Rob, 2020).
- In 2017, 98% had access to a mobile device (Rideout, 2017).
- In 2011, 4% of screen time for children eight and under was mobile, but in 2017 mobile screen time increased to 35% for children under age 8 (Rideout, 2017).
- Since 2013, the amount of time young children spend on mobile devices has tripled from 15 minutes a day to 48 minutes a day in 2017 (Rideout, 2020).
- More than ¼ of parents have downloaded apps for their children (Rideout, 2018).
- 72% of iTunes top selling apps are designed for preschoolers and elementary children (Shuler, 2012).
- In 2019, American teenagers spent 7 hours and 22 minutes a day looking at a screen (Rideout & Rob 2020).

So, now that you need to pick your jaw up off the floor or are nodding your head in agreement, this is what we know about kids today. I also know I don't need to tell you this because you see the impacts from these statistics in your classroom every day. Otherwise you wouldn't be reading this. Children are ALWAYS connected. As a matter of fact, they basically have a digital device as an additional appendage, and this begins at an early age. I could even give you data on the percent of people who text with two hands vs. one…but I won't. Let's not go there for now.

We can unpack how we arrived here by digging into a bit more research. While most of you are either Generation X (with birthdates in the 1960s- early 1980s) or Generation Y/Millennials (with birthdates in the 1980s-early 2000s), your children, grandchildren, or dependents are either part of the Generation Y/Millennial generation or they are in Generation Z. You may have also heard this generation referred to as the Net Generation. Generation Z, specifically, includes "kids," as I call them, who are born in the late 1990s or mid 2000's. This is where I will spend most of my focus since the NeXters from Gen Z are the ones you are currently teaching, and I am currently parenting.

This generation (Z), in contrast to previous generations, has been connected since an early age (as evidenced by my previous edutainment examples). Another way to think of the differentiation in Gen Z from other generations is by considering some hard parenting decisions your students' parents have to make, or decisions you have had to make. Do the parents of your students struggle with when to allow your students to have their first cell phone? I bet they do, unless, of course, you teach middle or high school. In which case, all of the students already have phones. Seriously, though, according to a Pew Research Study (2020), 73% of parents believe it is acceptable for children, who are 12 or older to have a phone; 45% believe it is okay for children between 12 and 14 to have a phone; 28% believe it is acceptable for children between 15 and 17 to have a phone; but only 22% of parents think it is ok for a child under the age of 12 to have a phone (Auxier et.al. 2020).

The intentions or considerations to purchase a smart device for younger Gen Z dependents are or were most likely for security and convenience. That might be true, but I'm sure Gen Z dependents have or will find many other applications for the device(s). Case in point, in 2017, the average American teenager was sending 3300 text messages monthly (Nielson, 2018).

Gen Z has experienced a lifetime of immediate communication and information. Therefore, its members expect instant access and resources. They are often referred to as "digital natives" because of this. They are very familiar with instant messaging, text messaging, email, smart phones, RSS feeds, tweets, and social media, but you don't likely need me to tell you this.

Of course, some research says that so much interaction with technology actually changes the way kids think. Literally, there is theory that constant exposure to technology changes the physical structure of the brain. One area I will explore is literacy and how our children are reading differently than previous generations.

Our brains, and especially those of our kids, process information that we read online differently than information we read in textbooks, which is why national education standards now include technical literacy standards. For example, students in the Net Generation have trained their brains to read by skipping around on websites, scanning for pertinent information. Science even suggests that their brains are being "wired" differently. In contrast, older generations are more likely to read from left to right and top to bottom as a result of our training and exposure to paper-based materials. Think of the differences in motor skills it takes to scroll down a page and slide it around on the screen as opposed to turning a paper page when reading a book. Can you imagine how these actions would engage the brain differently?

Access to a wealth of resources and information leads to a culture of instant information and speed. Consider how much information is on a webpage. There could be, video, audio, navigation tools, widgets with RSS feeds and/or advertisements, etc. Generation Z readers scan pages for the information they need and move to another website or resource if they do not find that information quickly by glancing at headlines or headers (Carr, 2011). This should also explain why Levin and Arafeh

(2002) at The American Institute of Research found that children who use the Internet complete their homework quicker than those who do not. Of course, they do.

So, it makes sense that Generation Z learns better in the school day and with homework by integrating technology. Older generations had Encyclopedia Britannicas, so we learned better with paper. Gen Z has never even answered the door when an encyclopedia salesman rang the doorbell. They wouldn't even understand a joke about it. If they are always connected to technology in their social lives it would make sense that they would be motivated in a learning environment where they are more comfortable and engaged.

I've included a quick reference list of facts about Generation Z that might interest you.

- Children in Gen Z have immediate access to publishing their thoughts and ideas through social media.
- They are master multi-taskers since they multi-task nonstop/
- They must be taught to be creative.
- 64% have constant internet access.
- They spend 8-9 hours per day connected to at least one form of media.
- 90% of secondary students have mobile devices.
- 20% of elementary students have mobile devices.
- They are the most independent generation because they have had less direct parent supervision since they have usually been in daycare as a result of being in single parent homes or having mothers in the workforce.

- Gen Z spends less time than any others in human history using conversation to communicate.
- They view marriage as less important, but they view parenting as much more important.
- They have more purchasing power than any previous generation did at a comparable age.
- They have higher rates of obesity.
- They are extremely social and group oriented.
- They are diverse and tolerant of diversity.
- They prefer game-like learning situations.
- They are more visual than other generations.
- Bad news—They live at home longer than any previous generations!
- Obviously, they utilize technology more than other previous generations.
- They view technology as a given, not a reward or piece of equipment. It is a necessity.
- They place value on the speed of their work, not accuracy.
- Their attention span is shorter, and they have a high dependency on technology.

(Elmore, 2012; Fedock & Young, 2013; Kinash, Wood, & Knight, 2013; Kotchick, & Forehand, 2002; Miller, 2011; Rozario, 2011; Schroer, 2004; Walsh, Branham, & Payne, 2013; Taylor, 2004)

Another consideration for teachers of students in this generation is this: there is a mass entrance of mothers into the workforce in comparison to previous generations, and the high divorce rate has created more dual career and single parent families (Taylor, 2004). Interestingly, even though their parents are working and being parents, they are the most involved parents of any generation. Generation Z is also known for being more sheltered than other children of a comparable age in previous generations. For example, Generation Z is more involved in recreational events than any previous generation. They are also extremely focused on grades and performance (Taylor, 2004). Can you say helicopter parents (I may not be Generation Z, but I'm a helicopter parent. So, I can get away with saying that)?

So, even pre-pandemic of 2020, we saw a different post-modern expectation in education than we had seen before. Parents needed to manage their time more wisely, and the drive to implement technology helped us face this challenge. Post pandemic, we have parents who have experienced the convenience, rather than distraction of technology, while realizing the importance of it in order to prepare their children for an even more competitive global workforce.

Knowing this generation, and how to educate them effectively, demands an understanding of edutainment. When they have had so much exposure to the online gaming world, how on Earth do you keep students engaged in your online course, especially since you aren't a game designer? Trust me. As an educator, you have mad skills and can engage students even more than something created by a fancy software developer.

SUCCESSFUL ONLINE STUDENTS

For years people have asked me what the profile is of a successful online student. Just like traditional students, successful digital students come in all sizes and colors and from all walks of life. The reality is, that the profile of a successful digital student is no different than the profile of a successful, face-to-face student. Roblyer and Davis (2008) found this when they developed the Education Success Prediction Instrument (ESPRI). White male students from middle to upper class families are more successful than other students in online classes. If you've been in education very long, then this should not surprise you. However, does this mean we should stereotype all white males that come from middle or upper class educated families and assume they will be successful while giving up on the rest of your students? Absolutely not. Children need all types of models for learning to meet their needs and learning styles. You will be amazed at the variety of children who are successful in online learning.

Simply put, the use cases for online learning are quite different than the use cases for traditional instruction. Many students who take online courses are more motivated to be successful, or perhaps the environment itself motivates them more to do schoolwork than the face-to-face environment for one reason or another.

In contrast, there are others who require intervention that is targeted to their specific needs. Also, there are students who are forced to take digital classes as a last resort, even when they may not be a good fit. I'm not making any promises. Digital education is not the magic bullet, but it is a solution for many students. Knowing that white males from educated families with a higher demographic tend to perform better, is simply a tool in the toolbelt as you assemble your diagnostic instruments to determine who might need more support.

When thinking about the variety of students who may be taking blended or online courses, remember that some may be in a full-time program while others may be only taking one or two courses. There are many factors to take into consideration when determining whether a student will be successful in digital education.

When working with a digital student, answering yes to the following questions can be positive or negative. Too many unfavorable scores will highlight whether a student needs additional support.

To Consider:	Favorable	Unfavorable
Does the student have time scheduled during the school day to work on the class?	+	-
Is the student working more than 20 hours a week?	-	+
Does the student have a device besides a phone (such as laptop/tablet) to dedicate to schoolwork?	+	-
Does the student have a supportive family situation?	+	-
Does the student have children or serve as the caretaker for siblings?	-	+
Is the student ahead academically?	+	-
Is the student behind academically?	-	+
Does the student have a few extracurricular activities?	+	-
Does the student have multiple extracurricular activities at the same time?	-	+
Does the student have Internet at home?	+	-

Please note that I didn't list a question about ELL or Exceptional Education. I want to be careful not to overgeneralize. I realize every child is different; however, consistently and over the years, I have found this to be true. Students that are learning English as a second language typically do better in a digital curriculum than traditional because words can be read aloud by the technology in the digital content, and images are present. They can also re-read text. Depending on the disability, many IEP requirements are included in digital curriculum. These students sometimes feel more confident in digital classes, but not all digital content is designed the same. These are areas you will want to investigate for your own ELL students and students with IEPs. In particular, if you have any voice in the digital providers being selected by your school or district, you will want to review the accessibility features.

The greatest skills I see lacking in unsuccessful digital students are time management and study skills/organization. The students who are not successful simply do not know how to plan or be self-disciplined with their time and organization. If an assignment is due on a specific date, they have not mastered writing it down or entering it in a calendar and organizing their work in a folder.

They also do not know how to create a plan that will allow them to work independently and complete a task on time. It always reminds me of teaching both 6th grade and 9th grade when I see this. I felt like I spent more time as a parent when teaching both of those grades than I did as a teacher. There is a special place in Heaven for those of you who teach those rights of passage years. Unfortunately, for the students who are taking digital classes for credit recovery it is always obvious that failure to effectively learn these skills is likely one of the primary reasons they are behind in credits and enrolled in credit recovery. On the other hand, sometimes, parents step in too far to correct things. Let's take a moment to speak to academic integrity.

ACADEMIC INTEGRITY

We have all had pushy parents, but what if that parent is doing a child's work for her online? Oh yes, it happens. Imagine grading and correcting an English essay. Then having the parent call you and after a heated conversation say, "I didn't make those errors...I mean Meg didn't make those errors." You can imagine how difficult it was not to laugh. Of course, I intentionally marked the paper up more than I would have, had I thought it was truly the work of a 9th grader, and, of course, I used red ink.

So, that was an obvious example, but questions around academic integrity are usually the first types of questions teachers and administrators ask me regarding online learning. Truthfully, you can identify cheating in the online or digital environment just like you can in the traditional environment. You can tell when a student's work suddenly changes. The real question is not about whether the teacher can recognize cheating in an online course, but whether the course is designed with curriculum that will allow the teacher to familiarize herself with the student's skillset.

If a course, blended or online, is composed of nothing but selected response activities, say multiple choice, then there is a chance the teacher would not be able to tell if someone else is doing the student's work. However, if the blended teacher is in regular communication with the student and during those communications the teacher discusses topics in the class, it would be revealed whether the student knows the material. In an online course, the same concept should take place during the weekly calls I suggested in Communication. If the student is making an A but cannot speak to anything content related during the weekly calls, then the teacher should have pause for concern.

Of course, there are other ways with digital curriculum to cheat than just asking someone to do your homework and then turning it in yourself. On a larger scale, there is the worry of paying someone else to do an entire course in a student's name. How would administration know or how would a teacher know if "Johnny was actually the one doing the work?" Ideally, the teacher is communicating regularly with Johnny, but in the event that communication with the teacher has been lacking, another way to catch students cheating is through server patterns. Recently, when I was working with a program, they noticed a computer with an international address logging in to a particular user account. As a matter of fact, there were two student accounts being accessed from this same location, which was a "Tutoring Service." In actuality, it was a service where students could pay to have their courses completed. I, in truth, think the company was astute to catch the abnormal IP addresses, and most schools or districts don't have the technology expertise or time to recognize these types of data analytics. I'm also sure that this type of cheating takes place regularly, which is why I encourage VOCAL strategies (Chapter 9).

If you are designing your own, or if you are on a selection committee for your digital curriculum, it is essential that the products you use include authentic assessment for the very reason of academic integrity. If there are authentic assessments, then teachers have the opportunity to actually see the work of students, not to mention to assess whether or not students are actually engaged. It is far less likely that students will be able to cheat in a course that includes authentic assessment or even project or problem-based learning strategies.

Other strategies to prevent cheating include testing students during your weekly 1:1 or offering live lessons and grading students for the work they do in their breakout rooms. Consider having students take tests in live sessions on camera.

CHAPTER 8

WHAT MAKES A SUCCESSFUL DIGITAL TEACHER?

Now that you have your resources and your curriculum, it is time to put them into action. Do you remember when you taught your first lesson in your methods class with actual students? Your first time teaching digital was much easier because: a) you have had loads of practice teaching, b) you may not be in person (no back to school dreams about accidentally wearing your bunny slippers), and c) if you are in person the kids are not paying any attention to you because there is technology. Sorry, you are not cool anymore. What makes digital instruction effective, though?

Using the acronym recognized by John Savery (2014), online instructors are more successful when they are VOCAL. This same acronym can be applied to blended learning as well (Visible, Organized, Compassionate, Analytical, Lead-by-Example).

VOCAL

Visible

As a digital instructor, you should make extra efforts to establish your visibility for your students. You want to make sure your students don't view you as instructors of distance learning courses were viewed years ago, that is as talking heads or sometimes even nonexistent. Your visibility will ultimately lead to your rapport with students. This is comparable to greeting students at the classroom door in a traditional classroom, putting your hand on their shoulders as you walk down the aisles, writing comments on their papers, speaking to them in the cafeteria, or telling them how well they played in the volleyball game the night before. It is equally as important to know student interests in a digital classroom as it is in the traditional classroom.

Visibility is specifically tied to your social presence in the classroom. Don't think of this as social media because that is a whole different ball of wax. Think of this as getting to know your students and showing them your personality, letting them consistently see that you are human. Interestingly, I've seen teachers who are introverts in the traditional classroom really develop a strong rapport with students digitally because physical presence isn't necessary to be "Visible" (and vice versa with students). Where there may have been classroom management issues in person, because of such strong visibility online, there are fewer management issues in the digital classroom.

In a blended environment, teacher visibility is easy to transfer because you have face-to-face time to get to know your students. In an asynchronous class, you may want to consider sharing your hobbies or interests on a syllabus; posting a welcome message that is a video to include hobbies or interests; timely response to discussion board comments and email; posting announcements regularly; and regularly responding to students with video.

Each teacher creates his or her own method for visibility based on the individual classroom and his or her own style. It is critical to be consistent and timely with all communication so that students know you are available. Timely and consistent responses also help students to feel respected and as though their messages are not getting lost in cyber space. Your presence provides the human element to their learning experience that is critical to their success.

If you are teaching an online course and have an LMS or other platform, you will also want to post regular announcements, at least once a week, at a minimum. In the weekly announcement you post for visibility, make sure to include something that is timely. This will allow students to recognize that your post is current. The post may be related to a current event or the current topic in the curriculum, for example. Ideally, this announcement will help the students relate to you personally as an instructor. You can do this by creating your announcement by video or perhaps using a text announcement and including something about a hobby or an interest of yours. The purpose of the weekly announcement is to make students aware that you are, in fact, a real human, and you are actually teaching the class. Obviously, if you are teaching a blended class, students will see you in person, so weekly announcements for visibility aren't necessary.

Organized

You have to be organized when facilitating a digital curriculum just like you do with traditional curriculum. Otherwise, you are going to go insane. Let me just put that out there. If you cannot locate files or instructions, then that means your students won't be able to either. This means they will be contacting you at all hours of the day and night because they are, hopefully, legitimately trying to complete their assignments. If you are in a blended classroom and the resources are not organized, then that means they will be off task, which will bring on classroom management issues. Yuck!

I don't know about you, but I like to talk with happy students and parents, not parents who catch me when I'm making mistakes, even if I am human. I prefer to have my students and parents think I am super-human, and that any mistake I make is an intentional one, only done to provide them with the opportunity for extra credit, if you catch my drift.

If you are teaching an online course that is provided by a vendor, then you should expect that the course meets standards as defined by the National Standards for Quality Online Learning, more specifically the NSQ Quality Online Course standards (Quality Matters & The Virtual Learning Leadership Alliance). Standard A1 requires that the course overview and syllabus be provided. If you are designing your own class, then this is a great place to start. Just like in the face-to-face class, in the online or blended class, students need a course overview and syllabus.

Having your class organized is a best practice, and it sets a precedent for your students.

You do this by having appropriate documentation such as:

- a scope and sequence
- a syllabus
- accessibility statements

In addition to providing documentation for students and parents, if you are creating your own materials for your digital class, you will want to name and/or number your lessons and units in a way that is logical to students. For example, you want the first unit or module to be named A with the following one to be named B. This makes it very easy for students to know the order in which to find course materials. Also, when asking students to submit materials, ask them to use a consistent naming convention for files so that you will know what files are. You should also be consistent with how you ask students to submit assignments to you based on your course delivery.

Course Delivery

If you are using a learning management system (LMS), then your processes for assignment submission should be easy to establish, but if you do not have an LMS, then you will want to identify exactly what you want submitted through email vs. what you want submitted in Google Classroom or SeeSaw, for example. Likewise, you will want to be very clear in which application students should view content and how it is organized.

Please note, I have only mentioned a few ways in which students can submit assignments and access content. You may have a website with content loaded for students to view in addition to school or system provided resources. Students, along with parents, will easily be confused with multiple locations to submit and view assignments, and it can be quite challenging for you to keep up with submitted work in different locations.

Compassionate

Although the original model for VOCAL (Savery, 2014) includes the term Compassionate, I often use Communicate instead (for more on this, see Communicate). Through the VOCAL model, compassion is developed because if you follow VOCAL, then you develop a rapport with your digital students. I cannot express strongly enough, however, that if you are teaching with digital technologies, especially 100% online, students feel a sense of security and anonymity behind the computer screen. They will, often times, open up to you and share personal information more willingly than in the traditional classroom. For this reason, and because you can individualize the learning so much with digital curriculum, it is critical to remain professionally compassionate for your students. This includes adhering to your organization's professional guidelines for interaction with students and parents. The acronym VOCAL will help you to implement all of the components to be a successful digital instructor.

Analytical

When I started Tennessee's digital learning program, I had the opportunity to work with a fabulous mentor who actually understood the relationship of data and digital curriculum. Quite frankly, the decision to have the online learning program in the division of assessment was purely political, but what a gift it was! Even though, no one at TN Department of Education understood it at the time, digital curriculum is driven by assessment, so it is critical that you not only assess the data based on your learner's performance, but that you also analyze and apply the data of your learners to instruction.

Are learners meeting the intended outcomes of the digital curriculum? Most digital curriculum, whether being used for blended or online programs provides you with excellent data to tell you if students are meeting objectives or assessment outcomes. Like I shared in Communication, timeliness of sharing this data is critical to student success. Fortunately, if you are working in an LMS or with a provider that is offering software, then the analysis is usually done for you. You just need to apply the data to your learners' individual learning plans and communicate it with students and parents.

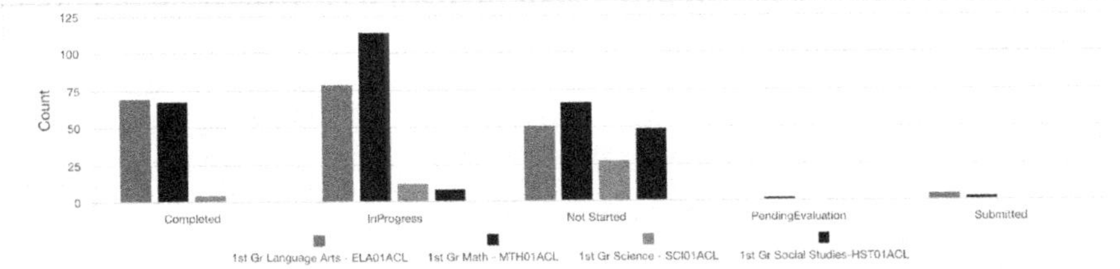

Drop Filter Fields Here

Count | Status | Performance

Course / Member / Objective	Completed	InProgress	Not Started	PendingEvaluation	Submitted	Grand Total
1st Gr Language Arts - ELA01ACL	69	78	50		4	201
1st Gr Math - MTH01ACL	67	113	66	1	2	249
1st Gr Science - SCI01ACL	4	12	27			43
1st Gr Social Studies-HST01ACL		8	48			56
Grand Total	140	211	191	1	6	549

Powered by FocalPointK12 2014-2021

Analyze also includes user and attendance data. You can learn a lot by determining when or if a child has been logged in. Either in an LMS or if you are using another software as a service (remember, this is when the school or district pays for a license), you can access user data. If you see that a child is logging in at 2 am for ten minutes and flunking everything, then *voila*, you have miraculously found the source of the problem.

Alternatively, if you see that a student is spending hours upon hours and still not completing the work or performing well, then you have identified another problem that you need to discuss with the student and parents. Obviously, having access to this sort of data, is extremely helpful when it comes to helping students succeed. This sort of data is invaluable in conversations with parents. One of the most common and enlightening conversations I have with parents is in response to how a student could be failing when he or she is "online" all the time. Data don't lie and have access to data that demonstrates when a child is actually active in a course helps parents to understand that if a child is "online" that doesn't necessarily mean he or she is working in a course or digital software.

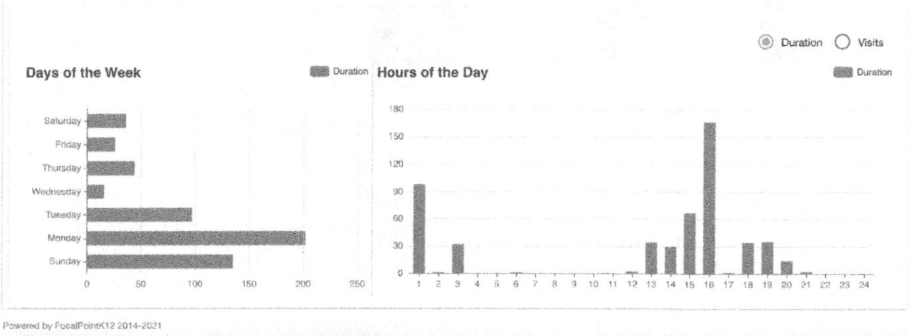

Unfortunately, and as I have reiterated a few times, free isn't really free, and you aren't the one who usually gets access to user data. So, while some resources may be excellent for supplemental activities, remember the limitations you have with them as well. Understandably, many teachers are told to "Go Digital" with no resources, and as usual in the education profession we make do with what we have. That being said, Analytical is just about data, in digital classrooms, students need to be self-aware and therefore have opportunities to self-assess regularly. This includes academic expectations, which is why in Communication I discuss the importance of the timeline and the way in which you provide feedback to students, but students must also be aware of your expectations for their own engagement in classroom activities.

Some examples include:

- How often do you expect them to log in?
- Are they expected to participate in discussion forums? How often?
- Are they expected to attend live lessons?

While all of this should be outlined in the syllabus (Organized), students should have the opportunity to self-assess and determine their level of participation in comparison to your expectation. This self-awareness/ assessment should help them to set goals and be more successful digital students (Hattie, 2009).

Leader By Example

My daughter, since she could talk, mimics everything I do. She speaks the way I do, and she interacts with people the same way I do. Being a parent is a big responsibility, especially when you have a "mini-me." Much like parenting, teaching digitally requires that you be very conscientious of your behavior because you are a role model in every way.

If you are teaching in a blended environment, and you use images that are copyrighted, students will then think it is okay to submit copyrighted work to you and thus other teachers. Teachers should always model best practices regardless of the medium. According to Savery (2014), students will take the lead from instructors on visibility, organization, and compassion.

According to Savery (2014) teachers should:

- Model behavior
- Reward students through encouragement/praise
- Discourage misbehavior with appropriate discipline
- Provide timely response to learners about grades
- Provide Instruction
- Provide questions to provoke higher order thinking
- Provide a structure for thinking and acting

By following VOCAL, you automatically meet the best practices Savery (2014) outlines for leading-by-example. These can be applied to a blended or online teaching environment. By applying VOCAL, you also build rapport, and provide effective feedback, that is actionable, goal-oriented, and timely. The key to being VOCAL is effective communication.

COMMUNICATE

As I said in the Compassionate section within the VOCAL strategy mnemonic, although the original "C: in VOCAL focuses on Compassion, it is extremely critical that you communicate regularly with stakeholders when you teach them using digital means. Therefore, I often suggest that there should be two Cs in Vocal: Compassion as originally defined and Communicate.

If you are teaching in a blended format, although your role should shift to a facilitator, this doesn't mean your presence, or your knowledge of each learner's academic progress, is of less importance. How you communicate your knowledge of each learner's progress and consistently encourage learning will depend on your rapport and the model you implement. Regardless, the consistency in which you communicate with your students will enhance the learning experience, and no matter what, don't forget to document any and all communication with students and parents.

This is the same for online classes, except, since you are not physically in person with students, consistency in communication is even more critical, as is documentation of communication, and modeling appropriate grammar (I know… former English teacher talking here). As I shared in Organization, you will want to communicate in a timely manner. Further, be sure to follow any requirements your organization has around response times. Some organizations require teachers to respond to students within 24 hours. Others may give teachers 48 hours. I suggest that you respond to students within 24 hours during business hours. This may seem intense, but from an online student's perspective they may get stuck in a section of the class at 9 am on Wednesday, if you don't reach back out to them until Friday, then the student has lost two days of instructional time.

Requirements for grading turn-around time may or may not be different than the communication turn-around times required by your organization. Some may be based on the type of assignment, so be certain to find out the specifics surrounding grading policies. For example, you may be required to grade short-answer response with 48 hours, but you may have a week to grade essays. For the purposes of visibility, I suggest that, if possible, you return student work no later than 72 hours. If I could wave my magic wand, I'd suggest you return student work within 48 hours. Remember too that in a digital setting, a student may be waiting for your feedback as a review for a test if the curriculum provider doesn't provide one. Some of the best online instructors I've seen have added a note taking requirement and their own reviews for students to complete before exams (if the software didn't include or require this already). This is based on visibility and the fact that students are receiving live instruction daily.

Giving students feedback has a significant influence on student achievement. This can be positive or negative, depending on how you do it. Does your organization have requirements for the type of feedback you provide to students or the ways in which you respond to students who are learning online? It has taken me years to find a model for giving students feedback, especially asynchronous students, that I really love and find effective. In my work with EdisonLearning, I discovered that they require their teachers to respond very specifically when grading student work, and their constructive methods for effective feedback receive national attention. I mentioned John Hattie (2009) and his work determining the key factors that had the most impact on student success previously. The EdisonLearning teachers have identified one of the key areas for impact in student learning from his meta-analysis of educational research—effective feedback, and they have put it into practice. According to John Hattie (2009) effective feedback has a .74 effect size. Remember that this means it is highly correlated to improved academic performance.

What makes the strategies for effective feedback that the EdisonLearning teachers are using different? They follow SEA, meaning they have to determine which of the three following areas to address in their open-ended feedback: Strategy, Effort, or Attitude.

- Did the student use the best *strategy*?
- Did the student use the correct amount of *effort*?
- Is the student using *positive self-talk* and/or *growth mindset*?

Adding attribution to SEA drives the effect score up to 1.42, which is really awesome (Hattie, 2009).

For example, you'd give feedback such as,

- Strategy—"I love how you used the transition word, 'however' in your paragraph What other transition words can you use on your next paragraph to strengthen your writing?"
- Effort—"Wow! I can tell that you put in a significant amount of effort when you created your project. I'm so proud of you for spending time on the details of the project and making sure to include all of the descriptive items required on the rubric.

I look forward to seeing the writing component of the next project where you explain how the great details you included relate to the theme. I look forward to learning more about why you selected the details you did."

- Self-talk/Growth Mindset—"Before you began the assignment you had amazing ideas and knew you'd do great. Your confidence and positive attitude will definitely serve you well as you begin your senior year!"

In addition to SEA, EdisonLearning teachers encourage continued progress towards mastery by providing positive reinforcement of both academic and online student behavior. They provide supporting information and clarity of why a student may have missed a question or points, and they provide supporting information to allow the student to understand the correct answer when they miss a response. The specific feedback they provide aligns to rubrics, and is targeted, timely, specific, and actionable.

Teachers utilize student survey data collected at the beginning of the term in order to personalize the feedback they provide. This allows them to key their feedback and what the students are learning to their interests and goals. Equally as important, the teachers receive training regularly on how to provide growth-minded feedback.

Students respond very well to the targeted and consistent feedback from their teachers, and the improvement in student work using their methods is documented. If your organization doesn't require a specific type of feedback, you may want to consider adopting a consistent practice like I described.

GROWTH MINDSET

Regarding communication, always use a growth mindset. If you aren't familiar with this concept, consider the difference in the following two statements made by a student about a diagnostic test:

I'm horrible at this. I will never be able to do this!

vs.

I haven't learned how to do this yet.

The first statement is an example of a fixed mindset. With a fixed mindset, you believe that the skills and talents you have are the ones you are born with, and these talents are what will carry you through life. Regardless of hard work, you are what you are, and you cannot improve upon your God given talents. People with a growth mindset, on the other hand, believe that given time and experience, they can nurture the skills and talent they are born with to continue to learn and grow, continuing to accomplish things in life. Therefore, with a growth mindset, feedback is always an opportunity to learn more (Dweck, 2008). Does this sound like edu-speak, or what? We learn through failure, right? So, all I'm suggesting is that you become cognizant of how you communicate with students and that we (myself included because I'm always working on this) practice what we preach when communicating with learners and their parents.

This means your feedback should always be formatted using a growth mindset. Rather than simply saying, "You're are awesome!" or "You rock!" include introspective feedback. Ask students questions about their work that will encourage self-evaluation. For example, "Why did you choose to do ___?" or "When X happened, how did this make you feel? How could you respond differently?"

Fixed Mindset	Growth Mindset
Great Job!	I love the way you did ____. How could you __?
Excellent!	You chose such a neat way to _____. What would happen if ___?
Needs Improvement	There are areas for growth. Do you have any strategies that would help with _____?
Incomplete	I see you are still working on some of the tasks. When do you plan to complete the rest of the assignment?
F (imagine big red ink)	I see many opportunities for growth on your assignment. Please schedule some time during my office hours, so that we can work together to take advantage of these opportunities.

BURNOUT

How do you do all of this without burning yourself out? Burn out is a real problem when you teach online or even blended, but let's get this clear. You are usually to blame for this problem. Yup, I said that. Your goal is to help students, and if you are teaching 100% online, each child may have a different schedule, which also means assignments get submitted at different times. The key is making sure you manage your own expectations.

What about rolling enrollment? Dare I go there? If you are teaching in a blended environment, at what point do you stop searching for better resources? The computer never goes away. One word for you: *Boundaries.* I realize this is much easier said than done, but you have to establish boundaries, or you will burn out very quickly. The internet never goes away, which means there will always be something sitting there for you to grade or look up or try to access for planning, regardless of the model or the type of resources you have (or lack thereof). This is especially true if you tend to be a perfectionist.

The first step in managing your own expectations is establishing boundaries, but how do you do this if the internet is active constantly and students are submitting assignments and emailing at all hours? Set specific times when you are directly available to students. If you are teaching in the blended environment, then obviously your schedule is set. If you are online, set office hours during which you are directly accessible. If students cannot access you during those hours, then make appointments that are mutually convenient within your scheduled business day. Speaking of, give yourself a schedule and a cut off time. If you are teaching online and working from home, you have to create a schedule for yourself or your work will swallow you up. Create a finite start and end to your workday. If you are teaching blended, especially if your school or district did not provide resources, do not let perfect be the enemy of great. Otherwise, you might as well stock up on Monster as your beverage of choice for the school year because you are not going to get much sleep.

Do not put an instant message app on your phone for students to reach out to you. It may be cute or fun at first, but trust me, it won't be cute or fun for long. You need to be able to disconnect from your work life. You need to be a mother or father, son or daughter, husband or wife, or just you. Go get a massage or hang out with friends. Most importantly, you need time to decompress, so that you can return to teaching fresh and with enthusiasm for the love of teaching.

Remember, you don't have to be perfect. As you will see when we discuss evaluations in Chapter 11, your expectations should be aligned to your years of experience teaching online or blended, NOT face-to-face. This is a new medium and a different pedagogy than face-to-face instruction. There are national standards to demonstrate the different skills required to teach online. Just like with the growth mindset, remember that we learn from our shortfalls. If mistakes are made, this is how we grow. Part of having a growth mindset is modeling it for students and discussing a fixed versus a growth mindset. When something goes wrong or doesn't work out well, then be open and honest with students. Ask them for suggestions for improvement. Remember, you are leading-by-example.

CHAPTER 9

THE BRIDGE: COMMUNICATING THE DIGITAL TRANSITION WITH PARENTS

In the late 90's to the early 2000's teachers were experimenting with blended learning models and integrating technology into their classrooms before there was a true definition for the model. As early as 1997, some schools were implementing online learning for students. But at what point did digital learning initiatives become school-wide or district-wide initiatives rather than a few teachers who wanted to experiment with technology to push the boundaries of traditional sage on the stage education of the 1950s?

While many found blended and/or online learning beneficial instructional models for students, probably until March of 2020, it couldn't be said that all school districts in the United States found a need for remote or distance learning. This was, of course, a result of the Covid-19 pandemic. In some instances, districts were immediately prepared to make a smooth transition to remote or distance education as the necessity became obvious, while others extended spring break or initiated an early summer break, depending on the community's access to technology and/or the school district's situation with digital resources.

Others floundered to try and find a solution for the educational needs of diverse communities while meeting stakeholder expectations.

So, how did you do? How did your district do? Assuming you were teaching in Spring of 2020, I suggest it is important to, not only self-reflect but also ask for feedback from families and students. Assuming you were new to remote/online learning in Spring of 2020, The Dunning and Kruger effect may apply. As I previously shared, this theory suggests that when our skills at something are low, we tend to overestimate our ability and confidence. Some good ole' metacognition for you (this is also why we have students self-assess and peer-assess). Therefore, while you may think you nailed it, this could be an example of Dunning and Kruger, and it might be good to get some feedback on your performance from parents and students in your classes, especially if you plan to teach remotely or online again. Be prepared and remember to apply your growth mindset.

Regardless of your individual performance, what most US school districts, schools, or teachers did not have in spring 2020 was a strategic district-wide, school-wide, or classroom communication plan for digital learning to communicate expectations to stakeholders. Had these communication plans been in place, then the transition to remote learning for all stakeholders, while still challenging because of the abruptness of the unavoidable transition, would have been smoother because a bridge of communication and expectations would have existed for all stakeholders.

Strategic District-Wide Communication Plan for Digital Learning

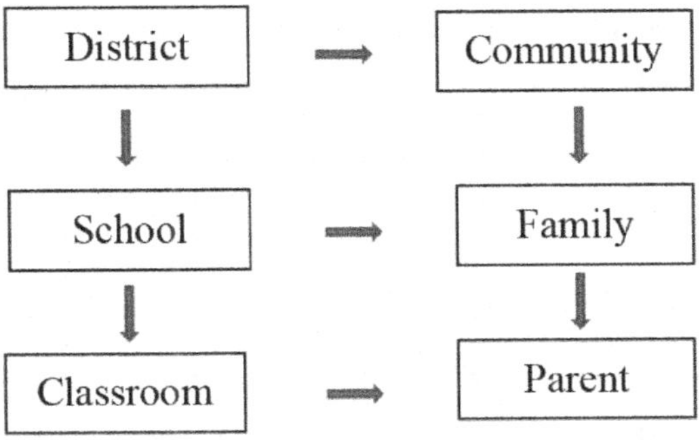

THE CLASSROOM TEACHER'S ROLE IN THE STRATEGIC COMMUNICATION PLAN FOR DIGITAL LEARNING

Getting the most out of this chapter requires that you understand how each different role in the district contributes to communicating your district's digital strategy to stakeholders so that you can begin crafting your own respective strategy for your classroom plan. What do parents need to know for a smooth transition? You should be familiar with the requirements of each component of the communication plan for digital learning: District, School, and Classroom (See Appendix A). However, you only need to develop and share your classroom plan. Someone from the district or central office, such as a Curriculum Director, on the other hand, would complete or participate in developing a district-wide communication plan for digital learning. An Assistant Principal would complete materials for a school's communication plan for digital learning. A teacher, then, would begin creating his or her classroom communication plan for digital learning based on the plan outline found in the Appendix in this book. Directions and suggestions for all three types of communication plans for digital learning are listed there.

The goal is for you to create your own communication plan for digital learning, but it is ideal that you review the information in the appendix that goes into all levels of the communication plan so that you can better understand the comprehensive strategy of the plan in your district and/or better understand how a classroom-level plan fits into the overall strategy.

As educators, we have been in the habit of complaining that parents aren't involved, but we are guilty of failing to equip parents with the knowledge they need to be involved in our digital transformations. I'm not suggesting that by creating a communication plan for digital learning you can suddenly turn the tides of parent involvement, but I do believe that we, as an education community, can do a much better job at equipping the parents who want to be involved in their children's education and supportive of their school's initiative to go digital. It is with the communication plan for digital learning that educational institutions can equip stakeholders with the knowledge and information they need to create a bridge between school personnel and stakeholders such as parents and students.

It is critical to understand that successful digital educators know and embrace the fact that parents are partners when building a bridge to success in digital communication plans. Here are some details parents need to know from the school as their children transition to digital education models learning.

What else can you add based on your classroom communication plan for digital learning?

- Internet security protocols
- Benefits of digital learning
- Communication preferences

- Discipline procedures/policies
- Class schedules
- School as a partner
- Teacher expectations
- Equipment responsibilities

COMMUNICATING HOW COURSES WILL BE DELIVERED

Once you know and can communicate effectively the plan for your digital transition roll out, the next step is to share with stakeholders how your courses will be delivered. Will students log into Google Meets, as they have been in previous years with Single Sign On (SSO)? This will allow students to click on a new app for their course(s) inside their Google Apps and "seamlessly" see their online courses. If there is an integration with the district Student Information System (SIS), then you won't even have to enter grades between the two systems. Parents will immediately see grades and receive progress reports. Talk about a dream! If you are a lucky, you are in a school or system that communicates clearly with teachers and staff and provides ample professional development on new programs before they roll them out. If you are in a big system or a system that doesn't communicate quite so well, you may be the last to know this information, and by last, I mean, … say the week after school starts. By preparing your classroom communication plan for digital learning you will be more prepared and will experience a smoother transition.

This sounds harsh, but often times by the time the school or district finalizes negotiations with vendors, contracts are approved by the board, and these projects get started, the projects are already behind schedule. Though not the fault of any one individual, it is what it is.

Don't hold it against your district or school personnel too harshly if you are the last to know of the plan to go digital. Most folks really do have the best intentions in place. That doesn't change the fact that the front lines are usually the last consulted, the last trained and the last to be kept in the loop.

What can you do in the meantime? Ask for the district and school's communication plan for digital learning, for an FAQ resource, and ask for a training schedule, to include the student orientation. These pieces of information should help you gather the details you will need. You can usually find administrative training guides online provided by the vendors as well.

CHAPTER 10

ONLINE SAFETY, OR IS IT?

When I first started The State of Tennessee's online learning program, I had to be careful not to use the term virtual. Instead I had to be conscientious and use the term online learning. You are probably reading this and wondering what the difference is. In 2006, many people associated the term virtual with games and inappropriate online behavior. The terms were not synonymous, nor was virtual a common term in education. Parents associated bad things happening to their children in virtual environments.

They were right. Bad things can happen to children in virtual environments, but bad things can happen to children in online environments too because they are the same thing. I know that you have been online and seen inappropriate images or language, be it intentional or not. For example, when I was teaching 9th grade English I researched the book *Animal Farm*, by typing the title into a search engine. I will not go into detail, but I can tell you I was mortified by the images that came up.

I was doing a legitimate search, and the images are forever imprinted on my brain. I had been married for less than a month, and I was twenty-three years old. If I, as an adult, who is now a supposed expert in online learning, made that mistake, then what will our children do as they learn to navigate their way around the Internet?

We all know technology isn't going away, and the convenience, the limitless resources, and the motivation the Internet provides for learning have more benefits than risks or consequences associated with internet safety. The benefits outweigh the risks if we are informed and conscientious when making our curricular selections. We just have to educate ourselves and our students on the best ways to avoid incidents such as my *Animal Farm* experience. Trust me. You don't want to see what I saw.

This is the little-known responsibility we have called "Digital Literacy." In addition to learning new instructional strategies for digital teaching, you also have to instruct students about digital literacy, and that internet safety is embedded in each of these responsibilities. As with everything, knowledge is power; and we cannot address digital literacy without the help of caregivers. If we make digital learning a team effort, not only will the education experience improve, but we will also be equipping our students with a stronger foundation in digital literacy which will positively impact their adult lives.

Before you can go to bat for internet safety, though, you need to know who your opponent is. Remember, children are online for reasons other than school. Also, they probably were online a fair amount before you began reading this book. Buckle your seatbelt because even as I write this both my parental and educator protective radar are in high gear.

PREDATORS

According to the FBI there are approximately 50,000 predators online at any given moment, looking for victims, yet we are encouraging students to complete schoolwork online (Child Rescue Network, 2019; Netzsmartz, 2019). I was watching my local news last night, and an online predator posed as a middle school teacher. Of course, children were open to chatting with him online when they thought he was a teacher.

Even though the internet can be dangerous, with proper communication between parents and teachers and with open channels of communications, along with expectations for children when considering digital education, the benefits outweigh the risks. Ideally, we, as educators, know what sites to choose and how to guide students when online. It is important to remember that in a 2018 Pew Research Center survey, 45% of Gen Z teens said they were online "almost constantly" and an additional 44% said they are they're online "several times a day" (Parker & Igielnik, 2020). That does not include time for homework which is why it is essential that many adults in their lives reach out to provide guidance on navigating the internet.

Many teenagers play games online, where these 50,000 predators can easily access their personal information. This is especially true since 27% of teens play games online with people they don't know (Child Rescue Network, 2019). Predators are smart. They will pretend to be younger than they are, acting as though they are kids or acting sympathetic to gain the trust of children.

Approximately one in five teenagers has received an unsolicited sexual exploitation online, and only one of those five told an adult (Pure Sight, 2019). Do the math on that. Twenty percent. All teachers should be prepared to have conversations with students who have been exposed to an online predator. Are you prepared to do this? What is your school's protocol?

If you can, think about this next statistic. One in 25 teenagers received a sexual solicitation online, where the predator tried to meet him or her in person somewhere. Think about that for a few minutes. That is at least one child from every classroom in America! On average how many classes do you teach? What is the protocol for this when a student shares such information with you? I don't know that our schools are ready for these types of conversations, but they are coming. I'm hopeful that we are able to respond swiftly and efficiently to protect our children.

Let me also clarify that online means a lot more than on the computer. Remember that when students are on their phones, they are usually online, and the 50,000 predator statistic applies there too. Most digital curriculum providers offer what is called "responsive" design, which means the content will adjust to fit the screen of a mobile device (think iPad/tablet or phone). This is intentional so that students can access their assignments on their mobile devices, which means they could potentially be accessing your digital content from their phones.

So, let's talk about phones, which are really mini-computers with GPS devices. When you were in school, you had to be conscientious of ruining your reputation with rumors based on your activities, such as going out somewhere where people from school might see you. Remember, it was okay to go hang out with your parents on a Friday night, as long as nobody from school saw you. Now, though, there is the issue with digital footprints, or digital data, that creates permanent pictures and documentation trails associated with text messages and social media. If a kid sends one sketchy picture, it can be forwarded around the entire school within minutes and even posted on social media sites.

In other words, one lapse in judgment can become a permanent scar, especially since 14% of students ages 12-17 out of a sample of 5,000 students *admit* they have sent nude or semi-nude pictures via text message . I find this statistic particularly interesting since 23% of those 5,000 students ages 12-17 say they have received nude or semi-nude pictures of friends via text (Patchin, & Hinduja, S, 2019). Either the same kids are sending out lots of pictures or some kids (9%) are forwarding pictures around to others.

Take into consideration that 73% of kids has a social networking site (Lenhart, 2019). The most common way predators interact with children and gain access to their personal information is through social networking sites. Imagine how quickly one poor lapse in judgment can ruin a student's teenage years or expose the child to a predator. Social media allows the network to grow drastically.

Say Angela sent Shane a risqué picture. Shane, wanting to be boastful to his friends, posted Angela's picture to his social networking site. Now his 432 friends saw the picture that was meant for his eyes only. Or, take into consideration the video of the female students performing oral sex on another student that was shared in Microsoft Teams during a live online class in Florida in 2020 (Travis, 2020). In addition to the students in the class who saw the video, did other students capture the video and share it? Once something is released online it never truly goes away.

Sure, there is Snapchat. If you aren't familiar with it, it is an app that supposedly deletes the picture as soon as the person receiving the picture opens it. On the one hand, this solves the problem of ruining your reputation as the evidence is immediately thought to be deleted. However, it increases the anonymity, which encourages risqué behavior, and it decreases the opportunity for parental monitoring. In other words, a student might feel safer sending a nude picture since the receiver cannot forward it, and a parent will definitely never know that the child did. Now, what if that nude picture was sent to a predator who was impersonating a kid the student's age? Because, guess what? Over half of kids sexually solicited online were asked to send a picture (Child Rescue Network, 2019). One thing you have to remember is that law enforcement officials somehow seem to always recover evidence when needed, even if it supposedly is deleted online. The truth is that absolutely nothing online ever truly goes away.

By the way, all of this is happening whether kids take classes with digital or face-to-face curriculum. Teaching them in a digital format, though, may provide an opportunity for you to improve their digital literacy.

WHAT SHOULD YOU COMMUNICATE TO PARENTS?

As I shared, it is critical to work as a team with caregivers. Truthfully, this stuff is really scary. So, I've included a list of ideas you can share with parents to help them not only protect their children's safety but also teach them how to interact, when playing, socializing, or learning in digital environments. Minding your manners has taken on a whole new meaning for Gen Z.

Create an open location for children to do homework or play on devices.

Recommend that parents **do not allow** computers, phones, tablets, or other devices to be used in private spaces. They should be centrally located, and screens should be visible to adults. For example, if they have a monitor attached to a machine it should be visible to anyone walking by when their child is doing homework or even playing. Allowing children to work alone on the computer in a room with no supervision is asking for trouble. Understand that when you are recommending this to parents, it may sound a lot easier than it is. As a parent, my daughter always wants to talk with her friends in elementary school on Facetime in her room. She has clear expectations, which have helped, but don't think it isn't an uphill battle. Older kids want to study in their rooms, and since they are using laptops it seems to make sense for them to take the laptop with them. In households where both parents may work or one parent or caregiver may work two jobs, this may not be as easy as it sounds. Therefore, I suggest you deliver this request with empathy. Sharing some of the statistics I have provided usually gets parents and caregivers' attentions pretty quickly.

As I shared in my previous book, as a former administrator, I have met with many parents who have been absolutely adamant that their child was online for hours the previous night doing homework. At the time I was able to pull statistics from the website the child was supposed to be logged into to do his work. When I showed the parent the statistics from the site, demonstrating that the child was only logged in for two minutes, the parent realized that "being online" and being online on the correct site were two totally different things. From then on, Jake had to do his homework at the kitchen table. Don't forget to make the data to which you have access your friend, especially if it can help diagnose why students are not successful in their online classes.

Not only do I recommend that devices for school stay out of bedrooms, but I also recommend that gaming systems not be in bedrooms for a multitude of reasons. Children will be tempted to play all night (enough said), and if those children play games online, parents will not be able to recognize signs of predators. Many predators disguise themselves as kids and connect online through gaming. From there, they befriend innocent children. Although you are the online teacher, and not the Internet police, if you don't educate parents about online predators and best practices, who will? So, if you have the opportunity to educate a parent on anything related to digital safety, please do!

BEDTIME FOR PHONE/DEVICE

What do I mean by this? I mean exactly what it sounds like. The phone or any other connected device needs a bedtime. Many teenagers take their cell phones to bed with them. No way should this happen. I can hear it now…, "But Mom, it is my alarm." Recommend parents buy their children a traditional alarm clock. I suggest having the child check in his or her device at a set time each night. This can be a central location for charging. This will prevent late nights and make early school or church mornings much easier. This will also prevent late night texting or pictures from taking place when judgment may be impaired by late night or early morning hours.

Many children will stay up late playing games on their devices or watching downloaded movies. Teenagers need their sleep for appropriate development. By requiring that the device be docked at bedtime, there will be fewer distractions. Additionally, there is inconclusive evidence around the electromagnetic radiation cell phones emit and the potential damage to the brain it may cause. Most children sleep with the phone by their heads, if allowed. It is best to limit this or turn the phone to airplane mode. This goes for you too!

ESTABLISH GUIDELINES

Suggest that parents are involved and establish guidelines for the sites their child or children are allowed to visit. For example, I would not allow my child to visit Second Life. I have had many people tell me there are educational uses for this application. However, each time I have entered, a flasher or stalker enters my page. I know how weird that sounds. This is regardless of my intent or the educational area I am in.

Parents can set parameters online at home. They can do this by applying a filter to their home Internet. There is also software they can purchase, or they can talk with their Internet Service Provider about setting up firewalls to filter pornography. If they allow their children on social media, they too should be involved in their children's social media presence, so to speak. Recommend that parents approve who their children interact with on social media sites and continue to have an open dialogue with them around their "friends." They should regularly visit their child's social media communities to see what information they have posted, and parents should discourage the use of web cams.

Help parents to understand that when children are using their own machines, as opposed to ones provided by the school, without resetting default passwords on their Wi-Fi router, anyone can access and see inside their homes or capture images from their web cams. Also, images are geotagged by default; that means anyone can see where they were taken. Imagine, an innocent tagline like, "our new trampoline" attached to a picture of their new trampoline in their backyard on social media, with default GPS tagging that tells predators exactly where their child lives.

Suggest that they discuss privacy with their children and that privacy settings are on! It isn't your job to be the internet police, but these are great tips to help a family as they transition to the digital environment, and providing this type of information to a parent will help build a bridge and develop your rapport as a trusted ally.

CYBERBULLYING

Let's not overlook cyberbullying. As I'm sure you know, kids can be very cruel. You thought you made it through the bullying years of elementary and middle school. Oh no…there is a whole new realm. One in three teens has been cyberbullied (Lenhart, 2007). It almost sounds silly to us since we experienced REAL bullying with REAL people on the playground or in the halls, but to this generation online bullying is just as real.

Remember the saying "sticks and stones"? Well, it isn't true. Cyberbullying is when someone makes inappropriate comments via electronic media about another person. Someone can make threats, mean comments, intentionally exclude or threaten someone. Think about it. How much easier is it to be mean to someone if you don't have to face them? When face-to-face bullying happened, you at least got away from your bully when you went home from school. Online bullying is committed at all hours of the day and/or night and it doesn't go away. If you don't know your school or district's policy on cyberbullying be sure to find out what it is. If you are teaching for an organization other than a school, make sure to find out how they handle cyberbullying. This type of behavior can come up in something as simple as a discussion board, so you will want to know the policy and procedures for addressing it swiftly and efficiently.

Please discuss the school or program's cyberbullying policy with caregivers, or at the least, make caregivers aware of what the policy includes. I suggest asking both the student and the caregiver to review the policy, sign off on it, and have them send you a signed copy at the beginning of the course. You should be fully informed of the laws and policies around cyberbullying in your state and be prepared to discuss them with parents should anything come up.

Report cyberbullying to law enforcement if it includes:

- Threats of violence
- Child pornography or sending sexually explicit messages or photos
- Taking a photo or video of someone in a place where he or she would expect privacy

- Stalking and hate crimes

Some states consider other forms of cyberbullying criminal. If you have additional concerns, you should consult your specific state's guidance.

If parents observe or are made aware of cyberbullying, make sure they know how to contact you directly so that you can serve as their advocate to follow the proper procedures with the school or program. If the individuals committing the bullying are from school, immediately notify school officials and ask them for assistance in dealing with the situation. Obviously, if you feel something illegal has occurred, then you should inform law enforcement.

THE PHONE

I find that many parents ask for guidance on when the right time is to buy a phone for their child. I'm including my guidance to parents on this very loaded question, should you find yourself answering the same question:

> *You pay for it, so you should monitor it. Are you prepared to monitor all social media accounts, texts and online activity?*
>
> *Part of growing up is learning responsibility and how to manage priorities. Children are not mature enough to set their own limitations with phones. This is a responsibility they must learn.*

Additional suggestions I provide to the parents include checking with your service provider regarding services that allow you to purchase additional services so that you can monitor usage, block certain numbers, control when your child's phone is on or off etc. There are also software packages that can be added to the phone to allow you to view all messages and images going in and out. Until your child learns the power and the risks involved with 24/7 access and communication, the parent needs to monitor and supervise all digital interaction to ensure safety. The statistics are startling, and remember I've only shared a few of them.

If caregivers ask your opinion, I suggest a "no phone zone" at mealtime. Taking online or digital classes doesn't mean a child's entire life needs to go digital. Suggest caregivers not allow phones or devices at the dinner table. Conversation is still a skill that is needed. I'm preaching to the choir because any teacher knows that parents need to spend time interacting with their children. The more meals a family has together the better the child's academic performance is and the less risky behavior the child will be engaged in (Council, 2018; Sen, 2009). Please advocate for family time and don't allow digital education to enable a lack of quality time with family at mealtimes. I can just hear kids saying, "Oh, I'm working on something for class" when they are really messaging friends. This goes for you too. Remember, your online class never goes away. Be certain to "turn it off" in order to give your family the attention it needs. Mealtime is a great opportunity to communicate about meaningful events or activities. Keeping open dialogue is essential for emotional growth.

SCHOOL COMPUTERS

Parents are really excited when the school provides a computer for schoolwork, but often times they are very hands off. They assume that if it came from the school, then all is well. They sign the necessary paperwork and are otherwise uninvolved with the child's interactions or use of the school's computer. There are some essential questions you may want to discuss with parents if your school provides learners with computers to take home. Remember, most of these apply to you as well.

- When students access the internet from home will they be "forced" through the school's network, or is it possible for them to get on home or other networks that may not have security settings on them? It is unlikely that students can access a home or neighbor's wireless network from a school machine, but not all school Internet Technology (IT) systems or IT Directors are alike. A parent should be made aware if a child can potentially access internet with no security filters via a school machine. If you are using a school machine and your internet access is running through the school, I suggest making sure you use a personal machine for anything nonrelated to school.
- Remind parents that there is a camera on the computer (if there is). Is it disabled? By the way, if you are using a machine provided by the school, this question definitely applies to you as well. If the camera is not disabled, I'd suggest covering it, as I would all cameras on devices in your home unless you are participating in a class discussion or assignment or are talking with friends or family, and the camera is in use. Why do I suggest this? For one reason, remember, anyone in IT can access your machine at any time if it has been issued by the school. Enough said. Laptop cameras can be covered with something as simple as a piece of paper, or there are specific gadgets that are sold for this purpose.

POLICIES

I have suggested some general rules that will allow you set up your digital workspace and help you advise parents in establishing a safer environment at home. But remember that it is critical to follow school/district or program policy and procedure. Each district or school will have different guidelines. Regardless of the type of equipment the school or program uses, every school/program should have an Acceptable Use

Policy (AUP) that you and your students should be asked to sign. If not, then you should ask to review it. This will outline the policy for Internet technology.

You may also ask to review the Online Safety Policy (OSP). It is likely that you and your students, maybe even caregivers of your students, will be asked to sign these policies or other policies specific to the school's/program's particular digital learning initiative. Ideally, these policies should be posted on the school/program website. If not, you may need to ask administration for them.

Here are some potential circumstances in which you would refer to the AUP or OSP.

- If a student is allowed to use a device from home such as a tablet or phone, review the documents carefully to determine who is liable if the device is stolen at school.
- In a bring "your own device" situation as described above, is the parent responsible for providing mobile data usage or will the child be allowed to log onto the school's wireless network? This is also a security question. On the school's network the school's firewall will be in place, which will include security. Is the parent responsible for monitoring security after hours? Are you responsible for monitoring for security during school hours?
- If cyber bullying takes place during school hours, even if the device is the student's personal machine, then will the school be responsible? What are your responsibilities?

All of this should be addressed in the Acceptable Use Policy (AUP) and/or Online Safety Policy (OSP), and these are just a few examples. Please remember this is still a new field, so you may need to specifically ask if you have concerns about topics that are not outlined or documented in the policy or procedures provided by the school/program. These same questions are applicable if the student is using a device provided by the school OR if the student is completing a homework assignment online required by the teacher. Let me give you an example.

- If Mr. Smith requires the students to post a response to a question in a blog that isn't part of an online class for homework, even if he is requiring it from home on personal devices, since he required it, is he required to monitor the blog for inappropriate comments?
    - If the assignment is required, then, of course, he should be monitoring it. Since it is a required assignment, it should only be taking place in a secure and safe location, as should be indicated in the AUP and/or OSP.

So far, we have talked about hardware and student behavior. What if a parent is concerned about an assignment? Is this different than in the traditional classroom? You should be prepared when teaching using digital resources that caregivers may well intervene more often. Why is this? Think about it. In a traditional environment, parents send their children to school; teachers close the classroom door, and voila, children come home brilliant. In a digital environment, children can work from home, and parents can, literally, see "inside" the classroom, either through live lessons or by clicking around in digital curriculum. For this reason, parental concerns come across as more critical because it is as if they are sitting in your classroom with you.

Additionally, in an online class, if a student is stuck or cannot progress forward either because of a technical issue or because the child needs additional instruction, the parent and child feel as if they are falling behind. They are losing precious time as deadlines approach. For this reason, it is critical to be familiar with your school or district's policies around timelines for teacher responsiveness.

Speaking of online curriculum, what if a caregiver doesn't want his child researching adultery online when she reads *The Scarlet Letter*? Or what if there is a sensitive family situation that your child may discover if he researches family history online? Speaking from experience, this can be challenging. I was team teaching a blended class where we assigned the students to research their family histories and design their own coats of arms. One of the students in the class found his biological father, a man he had never met and knew nothing about. Not only did he find the man online, but there were images of the man with his new family. Obviously, this took an emotional toll on the young man, who threatened to come to my house and burn it down, along with my computer (the primary target). To make matters worse, the young man's mother taught at the school with me and my fellow team-teacher. Ugg…Can you say lesson learned? I still feel awful that this is how the young man learned of his father.

Obviously, when we inherit digital curriculum or design our own, we have the best intentions in mind, and there is no crystal ball that comes with each student (wouldn't that be awesome, though?). Since you cannot be aware of all circumstances, or know a family's personal values, be prepared for a parent to ask for an alternative assignment. The additional visibility into your classroom and the anonymity of a digital class tend to encourage critical awareness of the curriculum. I've also noticed that requests for curriculum modifications tend to follow political trends. If something is popular in mainstream media, then you should expect to receive requests along the same theme with your curriculum. That being said, also note that sometimes it is easier to deliver more sensitive material face-to-face or through a live lesson asynchronously when you are teaching in K-12. I'd welcome the involvement, as it is something all educators want, but I'd also make sure to speak to procedures for requesting curriculum modifications in the syllabus if this isn't addressed in policy. You don't want parents asking you to change the reading assignment during the last lesson of *Romeo and Juliet* because they are sensitive to suicide, when, in fact, the child hasn't been doing any work for the two weeks you have been teaching it.

STUDENT PRIVACY

Let's talk about why passwords and user identifications, among other methods for data protection, are so important. We have a regulation in the United States to protect student privacy called Family Education Rights and Privacy Act (FERPA). This should sound familiar in relation to face-to-face education, and it applies to digital data as well. As a result, I'm going to go into a bit of detail so you will be informed.

Under the "Protection of Pupil Rights Amendment," (PPRA) parents have the right to opt out of any activity that would expose any "Personally Identifiable Information" (PII) for their child. PII contains direct identifiers such as family members' names or student names and indirect identifiers such as date of birth, place of birth or mother's maiden name. So, under PPRA, if a student is taking a digital course that requires PII, then the parent can request that he or she be given the course in paper format instead.

This would obviously be because the parent is concerned that personally identifiable information would be accessed by the wrong person or organization online. In context, an example of this may be that the parent is afraid an abusive parent could discover the whereabouts of the child by tracking him down online or that the parent is afraid his social security number would be stolen by a thief. These are, of course, extreme examples, but I use them to illustrate the point.

Under FERPA, the school has the right to release directory information, which is information such as the student's name, address, telephone listing, email, date, place of birth, pictures, weight and height of athletes, degrees, and awards. This is why identifiable information is listed in yearbooks and athletic or music programs. However, under PPRA, since this is Personally Identifiable Information, the parent, has the right to opt out by requesting that the school not include or identify the child if the parent has a concern. If you were ever the lucky one who sponsored yearbook, then you are probably familiar with this. This is all extremely important information to know when interacting with parents as you begin your journey teaching in a digital environment.

While FERPA and PII apply to all students in The United States, I would be remiss if I didn't highlight the California Consumer Privacy Act (CCPA), which went into effect January 1, 2020 and enhances the privacy of internet users. Specifically, CCPA applies to students or consumers (households) who file taxes in California, even if they live elsewhere part of the time. In order to meet the requirements of CCPA, a for-profit institution must meet the following five guidelines. This really only applies if you teach in California or if you are teaching a K-12 student who may spend time outside of California, and you work for a for-profit institution. What is critical is that caregivers of students California households:

- know your program's data collection practices, including PII, the source of the information, how you plan to use the information, and with whom you plan to share it
- are able to request any information you have collected on them within 12 months

- are able to request that you delete most information collected
- know your practices regarding selling data and be able to request that their data is not sold
- are not to be discriminated against because they requested enforcement of CCPA

This sounds pretty complicated, but you may want to review software as a service (SaaS) in Chapter 6. If you are looking for applications to supplement in your online classroom, the key is to remember that if something is "free," the currency is likely student data. If you are concerned about CCPA, you are better off to create your own activity than to take a risk. If you have additional concerns about CCPA, consult with your employer.

Much like CCPA, the European Union (EU) has a law in place to protect the privacy of its internet users by companies anywhere in the world. While similar in intent, many people think CCPA has the same regulations as the European Union's privacy policy, General Data Protection Regulation (GDPR); however, there are some discrepancies. For example, CCPA applies to *households* of California residents, where data could *potentially* be collected. Whereas GDPR limits its regulation to *individual* users and focuses on the specific data *processed*. Interestingly, CCPA does not apply to people or students visiting California, so if your online students live in Ohio and go to Disneyland for a week, you don't have to worry about CCPA (if you work for a for-profit), but if they visit Disneyland Paris while taking your online class, then the program needs to follow GDPR because GDPR applies even to visitors of the EU (regardless of non-profit or not). Note the difference in how the two define collected data too. CCPA focuses on any data capable of being associated with or linked to a household; whereas, GDPR defines data as that attached to an identified or identifiable person (Meyer et al., 2019).

Want a little bit of relief? If you work for a nonprofit, like a school district, then you don't have to worry about CCPA to begin with! CCPA only applies to for-profit companies. Knowing that many online teachers work for for-profit companies, though, it is imperative to include this section in the book around data. GDPR does, however, apply to non-profits and government institutions like schools, universities, and businesses. Since one reason students take classes online is for flexibility, it is probable that families may travel in the EU while enrolled in an online class, or perhaps you might take advantage of working remotely and do so yourself. For this reason, I suggest you familiarize yourself with GDPR. If you have concerns with either, definitely speak with your senior leadership, for I have only scratched the surface (Meyer et al., 2019).

While I am on the oh so exciting topic of data collection, one of the most debated topics surrounding data in recent years has been the controversial *standards and assessment movement* we have been facing. I'm sure you have heard of some of the concerns with Common Core and national electronic testing in the US. There is an automatic association between high-stakes testing and the Common Core standards, so let me clarify. The standards are one initiative, and high-stakes testing is another. Truthfully, while not at the forefront yet, digitized high-stakes testing is yet another hot topic for many of the privacy concerns outlined above. Politically, however, each of these has been lumped together. Let's separate them.

It makes sense to me that every child in America be held accountable for the same standards or knowledge, regardless of which state he or she lives in. In other words, if a student transfers to your class from a different state, the student should have been studying the same standards previously. Employers, colleges and universities could then expect that students who hold a high school diploma should all have been equally prepared for college or career. Believe it or not, though, prior to Common Core standards initiative, children in different states, counties, and even schools within the same county did not study the same things in the same grades. The breadth and depth of content or the topics and concepts themselves that were taught in each grade had the very real potential to be drastically different. This was true even between teachers across the hall from one another who were teaching the same grade or subject. My intent is not to debate the quality of the standards, but rather to explain the original concept behind them which seems to make sense and is really where the idea started. Albeit, it is a truly politicized topic at this point.

High-stakes testing is a separate topic from standards, and when high-stakes testing moves online, we begin to worry about the security of children's data. Robbing banks at gunpoint may be a thing of the past when something like ransomware attacks, where malicious actors or software can attack your system and hold student data hostage for fees, is now a real thing. But can you imagine grading multiple-choice tests for every student in the US by hand when it comes to high-stakes testing? Of course not, so online high-stakes testing makes sense from that perspective; however, the security of student data must be at the forefront of high-stakes online testing discussions. Unfortunately, there are bad actors or people with malicious intent who try to steal student data.

In December of 2020, the Federal Bureau of Investigation (FBI) and the CyberSecurity & Infrastructure Security Agency (CISA) issued an alert (AA20-345A) entitled, "Cyber Actors Target K-12 Distance Learning Education to Cause Disruptions and Steal Data." As a result of the increase in students learning online, and, consequently, bad actors or people with malicious intent, during the Covid-19 epidemic, the FBI and CISA released best practice suggestions for educational institutions and educators in areas such as networking, Denial of Service attacks, Ransomware attacks, video conferencing, and implementation considerations (Cyber Actors Target K-12 Distance Learning Education to Cause Disruptions and Steal Data, 2020).

Best practices for video conferencing recommend requiring a password for your meeting, discouraging students from sharing their passwords, and vetting attendees through the waiting room. Other suggestions such as how to mitigate Denial-of-Service attacks are specific to the program-level implementation and cannot be controlled at the teacher level. However, it is critical to note the involvement of the FBI and CISA in protecting student data as more students learn online (Cyber Actors Target K-12 Distance Learning Education to Cause Disruptions and Steal Data, 2020).

Statistical models and prediction instruments can be amazingly accurate. Who will have our children's testing data in their hands? Who is monitoring their Personally Identifiable Information (PII)? These are all concerns with internet safety. What will be done with all of these test scores, and will they be associated with user demographics or profiles? I encourage you to become involved in these conversations and to be informed simply from a data awareness standpoint, not to mention how these scores will be used to reflect on your own teaching.

Many states modified legislation to accommodate needs for the Common Core standards and for the testing to measure accountability during the 2013 and 2014 sessions. Creating the infrastructure to digitally test every student in the United States is an expensive and complicated undertaking. In 2020, some states were still not able to digitally test students successfully. I encourage every teacher to be involved at the local level, at the least, to learn how these changes impact the field of education. How will these initiatives move forward since our country has seen a groundswell in remote online instruction? I also encourage you to dialogue with the parents of the students in your classes to make sure they understand their child's testing data. It can be insightful information to provide a window into their child's strengths and areas for growth. Used appropriately and securely, the data can be a wonderful tool.

CHAPTER 11

WHAT'S NEXT FOR YOU?

Congratulations! You made it to the final chapter, so let's talk about your future and how you can be recognized for your continued learning efforts in the digital space. Although, I strongly suspect that we will see a major shift in existing education programs in the near future, blended and/or online teaching certifications are not very common yet. However, today's teachers cannot be effective in the digital classroom with one or two education technology classes, which is typical for undergraduate teacher preparation programs. Further, "Education Technology" classes don't compare to strategic class(es) specific to blended or online learning. As classrooms for educators, literally change, so will our teacher preparation programs.

In the state of Arkansas, for example, The Division of Elementary and Secondary Education, in partnership with the state university system and Team Digital, developed an online teaching endorsement to add to the existing face-to-face teacher licensure (Russel, 2020). While Arkansas isn't the only state to implement an online teaching certification, until there are more widespread opportunities across the country for training and certification, educators will rely on third-party training programs and interest-based organizations for training and for identifying best practices in digital education.

Although teachers have been required to prepare students for 21st century learning, for now, the resources available for the journey to blended or online learning have been somewhat limited. However, as digital education becomes more of a necessity, efforts to train teachers in this new pedagogy are becoming more common, and they are tied to school or program-based implementations. When schools adopt a new program or curriculum, typically there is a training included, but this training is usually basic product training, unless the school or district buys a specific professional development package from the provider. Because of this, often times, the training is a "one and done," leaving the teacher with a quick day of product know-how rather than a series of best practices to model and implement in the classroom. The good news is, there are additional training opportunities available to teachers that are becoming more available.

The Digital Learning Collaborative (DLC), for example, is an organization that was founded in 2018. It is financially supported by membership fees that come from organizations such as school districts, states, companies, nonprofits, and the like. DLC is managed by Evergreen Education, which has been involved in online and blended education for quite some time (incorporated in 2000). DLC is built on the work of iNACOL, the organization that originally championed blended and online education in the U.S. iNACOL is now called the Aurora Institute, which focues more on competency-based learning and policy rather than on the needs of practitioners, research, and best practices in blended and online learning.

The team that leads the DLC has been involved in digital education since its inception in K-12 in The United States. Some of the field's most respected leaders, practitioners, and researchers began the organization and hope to influence, provide resources, and validate research for practitioners implementing innovative digital learning models (e.g., www.digitallearningcollab.com; Watson, 2018). One way in which the organization is immediately taking the lead is by offering a minicourse that takes advantage of experiential learning to provide the basics of remote instruction during the Covid-19 pandemic. The intent of the course is not to certify a teacher in blended or online instruction. Rather the intent is to exemplify how the role of the teacher transitions in order to be an effective remote instructor. On average, the course takes 10-15 hours to complete, and each cohort is made up of 10-30 teachers. During the course, teachers participate in three synchronous sessions, and the remainder of the work is completed asynchronously in Canvas, a learning management system. The model of the course is much like students experience when they have "Live Lessons" along with independent work. There are five modules teachers must complete, each with an assignment that can be repurposed within the teacher's own remote classroom.

Teachers learn how their role transitions in a remote instructional model, how to develop community during remote instruction and how to develop rapport with their students at a distance. They are also exposed to curriculum development at a high-level and how to align assessments, to include formative assessments. Additionally, the content addresses some topics such as accessibility in digital curriculum. The culminating project for the program is an assimilation of their work, which includes activities from each unit that are all applicable in their own remote classroom (Powell, 2020). I really love that the topics addressed are specific to what teachers need as they transition to remote instruction, that the methods of instruction are experiential, and that the fruit of teachers' labors can all be applied in the teachers' own classrooms! This means there isn't a disconnect from the classroom, and as a teacher works through the professional development, he or she designs projects that apply to his or her everyday classroom.

Quality Matters (QM), another highly respected organization, that provides quality assurance in online learning, offers an online teaching certificate, amongst other quality assurance certifications in online learning for programs and organizations. In order to earn the teaching certification from QM, a participant must earn seven credentials from QM, one for completing each of the seven online workshops they offer. Each workshop is aligned to the QM Online Instructor Skillset. The seven workshops include:

- Gauging Your Technology Skills
- Evaluating Your Course Design
- Exploring Your Institution's Policies
- Orienting Your Online Learners
- Connecting Learning Theories to Your Teaching Strategies
- Creating Presence in Your Online Course
- Assessing Your Learners

What is unique about QM is that their programs take the perspective of the student, so the Teaching Online Certificate provides teachers with the background knowledge to teach online, and this information is presented from a student's perspective which enables teachers to empathize with students as they embark on their online learning adventure (Teaching Online Certificate, 2020).

Another organization that offers certificates for professional development that applies to both blended and online learning, along with many other topics, such as: digital citizenship, game-based learning, podcasting, social media, and internet searches, to name a few, is SimpleK12 (SimpleK12.com). SimpleK12 offers professional development in the form of videos, webinars, and blogs that are created by practitioners. For some of which, they also offer continuing education credits (CEUs) and certificates. I really like that teachers can select specifically the topics that they are interested in for their own professional growth. Additionally, what is really neat about SimpleK12 is the community of teachers they bring together. Through membership in their professional development offerings, members gain access to a teaching learning community of thousands of teachers, who collaborate and share resources amongst one another (SimpleK12.com). One thing my experience has taught me is that a team can accomplish a lot more than one person, so I appreciate their efforts in leading and managing a community that can share resources and solutions.

PORTABLE LEARNING

Obviously, a certificate recognizing your completion of a program from a reputable provider would be recognized for quality and rigor, but where do badges fit in? With advancements in technology, the concept of paper diplomas and certificates has begun to become extinct. Most of us want digital badges to recognize our accomplishments. Why are these so different conceptually than a traditional certificate of completion?

First off, they are portable, meaning they are digital, and we can transfer them as needed. Also, badges can be verified, meaning they are less likely to be forged or be inauthentic. Because they are digital, they have metadata that allows others to verify whether they are, in fact, legitimate. What types of data might a badge indicate? A badge usually has the data to tell someone the date it was earned, who earned it, who awarded it, what skills or competencies were required to earn it, and the URL. There are other optional data such as the expiration date, for example.

Badges are so popular that in 2011 there was a push for an open badge standard. Essentially, what this meant was that, when I was running Tennessee's online learning program, if I awarded a student in Tennessee a digital badge, it would meet the same standards as a digital badge that was awarded to a student from Georgia Virtual School, or even the same as a student from Michigan Virtual School, meaning that badges should be interoperable, following a common design standard. Think of this from a professional perspective, if you take certification classes from three institutions, each badge awarded should be verified using the same set of standards and therefore accepted by anyone. Technically, the badge must also "talk" to other badging systems. In order to do this, each badge must meet the same standards. Ultimately the project of defining the open standards belongs to IMS Global, a leader in interoperable technologies.

Currently, there are some pretty well-known organizations in this space, with whom you may be familiar, like Badgr. Have you seen people highlight their badges on their social media accounts? Badgr, not only offers badges, but it also provides opportunities for stackable skills which is when credentials and micro-credentials come into play.

When you are selecting a medical professional, you specifically look for someone who finished medical school, right? Ideally, if you have a problem with your foot, you will look for an individual whose credentials demonstrate an expertise in podiatry. Credentials tell us an area of accomplishment or expertise based on skills. I wouldn't go to a podiatrist if I was concerned about my vision. I would specifically look for someone who holds credentials in the study of vision. Similarly, if you want to demonstrate that you hold expertise in digital education, be it blended or online, then you may want to accumulate credentials or micro credentials. Ingredients are to a micro credential as pie is to credential. In other words, micro credentials are what make up the credential. Objectives may be the micro credentials, whereas credentials may represent mastering the grade level standards. In this example, competencies would even be more granular. As a parent and an educator, isn't it fair to expect that my child's online teacher has credentials in online instruction, similar to the expectations I shared about a podiatrist?

What is critical is that the credentials and/or micro credentials are not awarded based on seat-time, and completion of the unit of study is verified by a reputable organization. For example, if an accredited school awards credentials, then they have more value than if a school that doesn't hold accreditation awards credentials. Credentials awarded by IBM would hold more value than credentials awarded by a "mom and pop shop." This is because there is a level of standard assigned to the school with accreditation, and IBM is a reputable, well-known business. I'd have a lot more confidence in a surgeon who had credentials from Vanderbilt than I would one who had credentials from John's Chop Shop. This model is being implemented in corporate sectors, for education professional development, and K-12 and higher education.

The National Standards for Quality Online Learning (NSQ) is a project driven by a partnership between the Virtual Learning Leadership Alliance (VLLA) and Quality Matters (QM) with contributors from the online learning community. In addition to updating and revising the online course and teaching standards, which were last released in 2011, and the program standards, last revised in 2009, iNACOL (now The Aurora Institute), NSQ has begun an initiative to match professional development with the specific needs of online instructors.

As phase I of the project, NSQ has partnered with 2gno.me to create a portal that allows teachers to act as reflective practitioners, whereby they are asked to complete a short self-assessment that aligns with the national QM teaching standards (https://nsq.2gno.me). Based on individual feedback results, teachers receive personalized and confidential professional development recommendations such as recorded webinars and online courses. As the program grows, NSQ and VLLA plan to grow the professional development offerings to include blogs, infographics, checklists etc... I love that practitioners in the field developed this model, and the model itself requires teachers to be reflective practitioners which is an NSQ teaching standard!

As visionaries, this leadership group would like to expand the project to provide opportunities for continuing education credits (CEU). However, the various requirements by each individual state make this a complex endeavor, so there may be more to come on this in the future. While the NSQ project does not currently monitor its users' participation or completion of courses or webinars, the next phase of the project includes an external vetting mechanism that will notify NSQ of course completion. You might be wondering why this matters. Well, it is actually a good thing, even if it sounds a bit big brotherish. Think of students and monitoring their activity in classes. This is what allows us to give them credit, right? Adding this functionality to professional development creates the opportunity for badges/credentialing.

This is particularly of interest since this same future phase of the project also includes inviting professional learning providers to align their resources to the NSQ Online Teaching standards and link them to the 2gnoMe site (Nsq.2gno.me). Ultimately, this future phase of the project will allow educators to self-assess in order to determine areas for growth based on a set of national standards. Then educators will have the flexibility to choose from a group of aligned professional learning providers, who can potentially award badges towards a National Online Teaching Credential (Hamlin & Voelker, 2020).

Let me unpack this a bit. Essentially, teachers can take a self-assessment to determine what they already know regarding the online learning teaching standards and then participate in professional development courses only in the areas where they need to learn more about the NSQ online learning teaching standards (mastery-based learning at its best). You would only take what you need. What is even better about this visionary step in teacher professional development is that you would be able to select from which provider you take your professional development based on your individual needs assessment. Because NSQ approves the providers and the content in the program (because their content aligns to the NSQ standards), then their professional development content qualifies to award you a certificate or credential once you complete all the recommended professional development from your self-assessment. This puts YOU in the driver seat of your online teaching certificate, and you only have to take the courses you need. You don't have to waste time or money taking courses you don't need. Yahoo! Personalized learning for teachers!

BLOCKCHAIN

As you have been reading about these professional development offerings, I'm sure you have recognized that they are also models of digital learning. Without technology, they would not be possible. One of the primary benefits of digital education is that the student becomes the center of the learning model. By using blockchain technology, the student not only becomes the center of the learning model, but the student also controls his or her own documented record or history of learning, referred to as the learner record. A comprehensive representation of someone's learning record includes all of a his or her accomplishments that are *verifiable*. This includes certifications, diplomas, degrees, workforce development, or any other pertinent verifiable credentials a learner may earn.

Has it ever been a hassle to get your official transcript from your most recent university? I just hope you didn't have an outstanding parking ticket that earned interest from 1999 when you tried to get your transcript! If you did, then you definitely learned who was in control of YOUR learning record. However, imagine, if you will, that your academic records live in one central location that you control, where you determine who gets access, not the university or company where you earned your certification. After all, it is YOUR learning record, and the university has already certified your transcript and issued it, right? Shouldn't you now be in control of who receives your data?

Should you also be in control of who sees and receives your learning data when you earn certificates for additional training? To dig deeper into what a verifiable credential is, let's take the credentialing explanation from earlier a step further. With credentialing, a third party, like QM, would issue you a certificate for completing specific requirements of a course successfully. Let's say you earn an online teaching certificate from QM, and they credential it. In other words, they verify that the certificate is, in fact, from them; therefore, it is a valid certificate, not something you bought from your cousin's friend in some back alley in the city. If an organization like QM or any other organization that offers training were to implement blockchain technology, then they would push their credential to your personal "chain." From there, you would choose with whom to share a link to your "chain." The data on your "chain" would always live there. Once published it will never go away, but you choose with whom to share it. In other words, YOU, the learner, are in control of your learning record, and you do not need to request your data from institutions.

Blockchain is a way to distribute information or data on a de-centralized ledger. Financial institutions and medical institutions use this technical model to store data securely. Just like health care providers, thought leaders in education are beginning to explore ways in which the model can apply to education professionals. Essentially, you have an app, which is often referred to as a wallet, on your device that holds a "key" or a password to unlock your information. You can choose to share your data or files with certain people by sending them links to specific information on your chain. What is important is that any credential you have would have been validated and awarded by a third party. Otherwise, it wouldn't be on your chain (this is how blockchain works). Without this validation process, data on the blockchain, such as credentials or certifications, wouldn't hold any value because it would be equivalent to your very proud mom saying what a wonderful teacher you are!

In a blockchain ledger, a "miner" has to validate any data awarded to your chain before it is added. That is what makes the technology so secure. This is why we are beginning to see student transcripts awarded to a blockchain. The concept of life-long learners can be documented in one place without the hassle of a paper. The digital learning record then follows the learner from high school, to college and career and beyond. I like to refer to blockchain as credentialing on steroids!

I bring up blockchain because there is professional development on digital teaching available that is credentialed and awarded on blockchain. We are in the beginning phases of applying blockchain technology to education, but as organizations such as USDOE begin their Education Blockchain Action Network in order to collaborate on the uses of blockchain in education, you should take advantage of the technology for your own professional development. This will enable you to be on the cutting edge of digital education. More importantly, as you complete this book, it is critical that you parallel student learning with your own. How will the advent of blockchain in education change how we offer and implement digital education, not only for students, but also for teacher professional development?

TEACHER EVALUATION

What does all this mean for teacher evaluation? How does your administrator do a walk-through if your classroom isn't in a physical space to actually walk through? When stakes are high, when you are being observed, for example, it is pretty frightening to try something new. Imagine going from being the highest-level teacher in your state to scoring very low simply because you taught with a new model that you were required to use. Not fun! I'm not sure I'd be very supportive of change if I happened to be in this situation either. We have to allow teachers to fail with new technology and new instructional models in order to allow them to grow and succeed. In so many ways your first days teaching blended or online will be reminiscent of your first days in the classroom. Don't worry. It won't last long. But you do have to be willing to get out of your comfort zone, and administrators have to provide appropriate professional development, leadership, and support.

Administrators or peer evaluators need to consider that there are so many more and different variables at play when comparing digital and face-to-face programs. An evaluation of a teacher in an online or blended classroom does not compare to one in a face-to-face classroom. In reality this is like comparing apples to oranges. It is quite frankly a different teaching model; therefore, a different rubric with different expectations should be used. Teachers and administrators should also take into consideration that students enroll in online classes for a variety of reasons, which means their circumstances and capabilities are likely very different than traditional students. Flexibility is one of the drivers of online education. Because of this, without sophisticated statistics, comparing face-to-face and online students isn't realistic. For example, an online student may complete two-weeks' worth of work in one week in an effort to get ahead because he or she has an upcoming competitive event and will be unable to focus on schoolwork. Whereas, a student in a face-to-face classroom is bound by the schedule of the teacher. Because of this, attendance cannot be compared, for example, because the online student may not be logging in every day like the student in the face-to-face environment, but his or her work is completed on time, if not early. To penalize the online student for attendance would not be logical.

Because standards for teaching blended and online instruction are different than those for traditional instruction, teachers and evaluators should be certain to clearly define the standards for evaluation along with outcome measures and expectations before any evaluative measures take place. Teachers should also communicate about any challenges they foresee when evaluating blended and/or online classes. For example, I expect program maturity and teacher experience to impact the evaluation process. If the school is in the first year of the digital program, then an administrator cannot hold teachers accountable to a model that is in its fifth-year of implementation. Certainly, it is a great idea to strive for an excellent model if a teacher or administrator has found one that fits the school's vision, mission, and population. Remember, however, in your first year of implementation, you will be figuring out bugs in the system, learning shortcuts, learning tips and tricks for classroom management and software implementation. You will also be able to test your ideas and determine what works best with students regarding engagement and motivation.

Another factor to consider is the vendor maturity:

- How long has the particular software the school has adopted been on the market?
- How long has the individual teacher used the software the school has adopted?

If you are working with a software or curriculum that has been used by other schools and programs for multiple years, then you can feel confident that it has been vetted. Newer curriculum, like textbooks, may have errors that you need to vet. This isn't uncommon for new releases in digital curriculum. Even if you are working with a vendor that has worked in digital education for many years, when they release new content, there may be a bug or content error or even a glitch that happens when high numbers of students begin using it. If this is the case, then you will need to submit feedback to the vendor. Additionally, even if the product is perfect, the first time you use any new curriculum, paper or digital, it is harder and more time consuming than something you've used multiple years or multiple times. This is why vendor maturity has to be taken into consideration for online or blended teacher evaluation. I suggest scaffolding evaluations much like you do student instruction. Through evaluation versioning, as the teacher becomes more experienced with a digital curriculum or model, expectations increase. This can be managed through a rubric versioning process. For example, rubric 1.0 would be for a novice digital teacher, regardless of face-to-face years of experience. Rubric 2.0 would be for a more experienced digital teacher and so forth and so on. Each rubric would have higher expectations.

One model that I have found successful that uses the versioning I outlined for online instructors is to implement formative or informal walkthroughs based on monthly professional learning community (PLC) topics, which are usually a focus of an instructional standard (NSQ). This creates an opportunity to focus on improvement over a month-long period, which includes self and peer observation. Walk-through expectations increase in depth and breadth of the standard based on the maturity of the teacher's experience with the online program. Summative observations are a cumulative result of the walkthroughs as well as goal setting and a formal "dog and pony" show/observation, if you will. This same model can be adopted for the blended classroom. The individual goal setting is based on feedback from the Oliver's Online Practice Profile, whereby participants take a self-assessment that is aligned to the NSQ teaching standards as well as Oliver's Framework for Online Instruction (2014). Confidential personalized results inform the teacher of areas for growth in online learning based on national standards. This data helps teachers and administrators set realistic targets for growth and determine goals for professional development. It is important that educators not only implement best practices for digital instruction but to also model them.

We are at the tipping point in education, where, as a result of the Covid-19 pandemic, digital education became a definitive part of daily education for students in grades K-12. Will the pandemic drive the rebirth or Renaissance of the American education system? We have seen over and over that progress and innovation are born of change. Change, especially in education is very slow and difficult; however, because of the 2020-2021 Covid-19 pandemic, change in the way in which education is offered to students the world is inevitable. Because of the necessary and immediate solutions to offer children education during the pandemic, parents have become more aware of choices for which they can advocate within public education; the constraints of seat-time are being recognized; and a shortage of qualified educators is creating a gig economy for teaching opportunities, to name a few. All of these changes are driven by technology. How will you respond as you have the chance to advocate for digital education rather than continuing with the offering of an educational model that was designed for the Industrial era?

ABOUT THE AUTHOR

With over fifteen years of leadership experience in digital education, Dr. Wendy Oliver has worked with twelve states, focusing her consulting work on implementing innovative learning models and creating life-long learning experiences. Throughout her career, which began as a teacher, Wendy has had the opportunity to develop and pioneer district and state-wide digital learning programs, beginning in The State of Tennessee. She also served as the Chief Learning Architect for Arizona State University's digital 9-12 charter school and currently serves as the Chief Learning Officer for Edison Learning.

Wendy created Oliver's Frameworks for Blended and Online Instruction and subsequent software that allows teachers to self-assess their educational knowledge in each respective environment, where they also receive credentialed, professional development pathways.

Dr. Oliver focuses her energy at the national level developing best practices in digital education and consulting with practitioners in order to build successful digital learning models. She serves on several national boards and recently co-led the rewrite of the national online teaching.

In 2019 she released her first book, *Not Your Mama's Classroom: What You Need to Know as a Parent About Your Child's Digital Education.*

As someone who loves to learn, no matter which hat she's wearing, her goal is simple—to empower learners.

DrWendyOliver.com
@oliver_dr

OTHER RESOURCES FROM DR. OLIVER

Not Your Mama's Classroom: What You Need to Know as a Parent About Your Child's Digital Education includes: actual pedagogy, successful student and teacher profiles, developing original curriculum, deconstructing standards, creating rubrics, communicating with students and parents, live lessons, assessments, exceptional education/accessibility, and online safety.

Available at DrWendyOliver.com.

APPENDIX

COMMUNICATION PLAN FOR DIGITAL LEARNING —THE BRIDGE BETWEEN STAKEHOLDERS

Although, I referenced your classroom components of a communication plan for digital learning within the text of the book, Appendix A represents a holistic view of the communication plan for digital learning so that you, the teacher, can better understand how your classroom plan fits into the bigger picture. Most districts do not have a communication plan for digital learning, so please feel free to share this plan in its entirety with your stakeholders. It is intended as a resource and can even be used as a foundational template.

While we complain that parents aren't involved, we aren't equipping parents with the knowledge they need to be involved in our digital transformations. I'm not suggesting that by creating a communication plan for digital learning you can suddenly turn the tides of parental involvement. I do, however, believe that you can do a much better job of equipping the parents who want to be involved in their children's education and supportive of the school's initiative to go digital. It is with the communication plan for digital learning that educational institutions can equip stakeholders with the knowledge and information they need to create a bridge between school personnel and stakeholders such as parents and students.

Most US school districts, schools, or teachers did not have a district-wide, school-wide, or classroom communication plan for digital learning to communicate expectations to stakeholders in spring of 2020 when the pandemic hit. Had these plans been in place, then the transition to remote learning for all stakeholders, while still challenging because of the abruptness of the unavoidable transition, would have been smoother because a bridge of communication and expectations would have existed for all stakeholders.

DISTRICT-WIDE COMMUNICATION PLAN FOR DIGITAL LEARNING

The district-wide communication plan for digital learning sets the expectation for all of the schools in the district; therefore, it provides guidance for each administrator's plan and for all teachers' individual Communication Plans for Digital Learning. The goal of the plan should be to outline all policy that is necessary to create a bridge of communication around the digital implementation model at the district-level and provide procedures for key stakeholders.

School/District Title of the Plan

The district-wide communication plan for digital learning should specifically name the type of program the district intends to implement, regardless of the autonomy each building may have for implementation. For example, are you going to call the program your "one-to-one initiative," your "distance learning plan," or something more closely related to the community such as "Daisy Digital Model"? Regardless of the title, it should indicate the medium of learning. The examples provided previously suggest either one-to-one, online/distance, or digital all based on their respective titles.

Definition

Once titled, a definition of the program that all stakeholders understand needs to be included. "We are beginning a personalized, digital learning program for all students this year!" Well, that really tells a parent nothing unless they are involved daily in education conversations. Parents and community members need to hear more specifically what you are doing.

We are starting a one-to-one digital learning initiative in 2021, where every student is assigned his or her own computer. Since each child will be provided a computer by the school, that he or she will be allowed to take home, teachers will be assigning classwork and homework online. Some of our classrooms will take advantage of online learning, where students complete learning using the internet. In other classrooms, teachers may use a blended model, where they use both online resources and traditional classroom instruction, yet in other classes teachers may ask students to watch videos of lectures at home in order to prepare for class the next day (the flipped classroom).

Devices

Although you have made stakeholders aware that you are going one-to-one, what does this mean? In other words, if I own a local pawn shop, for what should I be on the lookout? You should include an explanation of what types of machines you are providing students and why.

X School District is providing individual students with Chromebooks beginning in August 2021. Chromebooks have become the most popular devices in education for many reasons including but not limited to the fact that they are durable, easy to use, have a long battery life, and meet requirements outlined by our teachers for their needs for digital instruction.

In this section be certain to include any expectations (or links to expectations) such as any agreements that students must sign such as insurance for devices or agreements regarding damage, theft, or loss. Include the district acceptable use policy (AUP), along with a brief explanation of what it is, and include the district internet safety policy.

Access

If there is a percent of your district that does not have Internet access, then identify what that percent is, and provide suggestions or options for that community. For example, you may say something like:

We are aware that X% or 415 students in our community do not have home internet access. Technology Services is working with those families to provide alternative options such as: working with community partners to provide internet access, removing barriers to offer access on school campus, securing community locations where Wi-Fi is available, and/or providing alternative learning packets.

District Security

This section of the Digital Communication Plan is critical to parents. If you have an existing Information Technology Security Plan, then I suggest linking to it here. If you do not, then I suggest you work with your IT department to communicate, in laymen's terms, what filters you have on the devices being used in your program. For example, if you use Kahoot, then explain what Kahoot does in this section of the Communication Plan for Digital Learning.

It is critical, depending on how your machines are configured, to explain to stakeholders that when at school, Internet activity takes place through the school firewalls, but from home, students may be accessing the internet through their home network. This means Mom, Dad, Grandma, Grandpa, Aunt, Uncle, sibling or friend's parent may need to adjust router settings. It cannot be assumed that someone comfortable and knowledgeable with technology is at home, regardless of the child's age or situation.

It would not be a bad idea to ask your IT team to include a brief tutorial on how to do this in this section of your Digital Communication Plan. You may even want to consider something simpler. Many parents are not aware of how to turn on SafeSearch in Google, for example (Go to your Google settings and select "Safe Search"). Even something as simple as this is critical for stakeholders to know as you start this new model, for children may need to use a parent's machine from time-to-time.

Teachers

Teachers are stakeholders in this new model, just as much as parents and students are. While there is some information that you may not want to communicate on a document that has all stakeholders as the intended audience, it is critical that shared information regarding policy and procedure for teachers, where appropriate, also be included in the communication plan for digital learning. For example, what is the district-level expectation of teachers in the transition to digital? What is the vision of the teacher's role in this new learning model? Does it vary depending on grade level? Teachers will need to look to this statement for guidance as they determine how to take advantage of the technology being provided by the district in their new pedagogical models.

For many teachers this transition can be very frightening. Many may feel as if they are being replaced or seen as less valuable, when in fact, the opposite is the case. The technology is being provided to equip them with more data and tools to diagnose learning. This provides them with more tools to provide recommendations and solutions for students.

No one complains when doctors have more technology to diagnose medical needs or to operate. As a matter fact, people are grateful because the more tools a surgeon has, the more likely the surgeon can find the problem(s) and recommend solutions. Teachers need to recognize digital initiatives for what they are, equipping them to do their jobs even better. Just like in the medical profession, will the district support teachers by providing professional development? Parents would also like to know if the district is supporting teachers, for handing children computers and wishing teachers, "Good Luck!" does not exactly indicate a well-thought out plan for success with your district's digital initiative.

Social Media Images in the Classroom

Most likely, your Human Capital division already has a social media policy for employees that explains the repercussions of posting inappropriate content on social media. While you may prefer to put it in the employee handbook rather than in the communication plan for digital learning, please reiterate it as you transition to a digital program. As teachers begin making the transition to digital or remote learning, they get excited and are very proud to share the work of their students.

Unless your legal division advises differently, I highly recommend that you include something similar to the following if it does not already exist in your employee handbook as well,

Teachers may only include pictures of students whose parents/guardians have signed the photo release form. They may only post images of students on sites that require a user ID and password available only to families. Families must be required to opt-in to the opportunity for the digital community, where pictures of students are posted.

Using social media can be a great way to build community in a remote setting and thereby build the communication bridge between parents, students, and teachers, but it can also be like opening Pandora's box. Therefore, you will want to offer some additional communication guidelines for teachers' district-wide communication plan for digital learning. For example, at the district level, teachers are expected to use professional judgement when contacting students through social media. Many students and parents will "add" teachers via social media, especially if school is remote. This adds to their interaction and creates a stronger rapport.

For older students, teachers may see concerning behavior on student social media accounts and vice versa. This may also be the case with parents of students. What is the district policy on interacting via social media? Teachers may be afraid to not accept "requests" from social media from certain members of the community, but if the 2021 communication plan for digital learning states that teachers should not fraternize with students or parents of current students on social media other than school approved accounts, then teachers can use the plan as a reference. This would, therefore, leave them with the option of declining and referencing the communication plan. A statement such as this would still allow families to build rapport and create a bridge based on a specific platform that only current families who have opted into have access.

It is common to see guidance around messaging in this section of a communication plan for digital learning. Parents appreciate seeing the guidance provided, and teachers appreciate the specific guidance. For example, do you want to state that direct communication should be age appropriate and specific to the student's education? Do you want to require that parents be copied on all communication to elementary and middle school students, unless parents opt-out? You will see some plans that do not require parents of high school age students to opt-out of receiving copies of communications from teachers, but I strongly suggest you make this required.

FAQ

It is always important to have a frequently asked questions (FAQ) section of any plan. It is also critical that you have several stakeholders read the plan and the FAQ to make sure you avoid education jargon. It is likely that you will have several team members contribute to this plan, and you will want one person to edit it so that the plan reads with a consistent voice.

Plan Location and Formatting

Please note the literacy level of your community when writing your plan. If your community has an average of a 7th grade literacy level, then a plan written at the 12th grade level doesn't serve much of a purpose. It is critical that the formatting of the document be easy to navigate and that it be located in an easy to identify and locate place on your website. Additionally, the user should be able to click on the name of each school and visit each School-Level Communication Plan for Digital Learning from the District-Wide Communication Plan for Digital Learning.

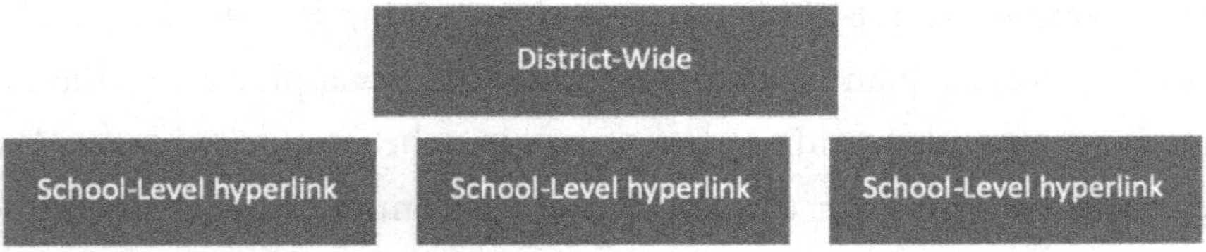

SCHOOL-LEVEL COMMUNICATION PLAN FOR DIGITAL LEARNING

The district-wide communication plan for digital learning sets the expectation for all of the schools in the district. Therefore, it provides guidance for each administrator's plan and for all teachers' individual Communication Plans for Digital Learning. The goal of the district plan should be to outline all policy that is necessary to create a bridge of communication around the digital implementation model at the district-level and provide procedures for key stakeholders.

The School-Level Communication Plan for Digital Learning should serve as a guide and play a liaison role between the classroom teacher's plan and the district's plan. There are many building-level decisions that must be made in order to implement a successful digital learning plan, and stakeholders look to the School-Level Communication Plan for Digital Learning to illustrate this information.

School-Level Model

Just as the district defined the overarching model in the district plan as 1:1, distance, digital etc...., each school needs to define its personalized model. A district-wide 1:1 model looks very different in an elementary school than it does in a high school, for example. How are you planning to implement a digital learning model in your school? What makes it any different than handing children a computer and telling their teachers to use online resources rather than textbooks?

In this section you should go beyond the definition of the model (e.g., 1:1) since this was done in the district-level plan. Think of this section as the "what" of the document. For example, are you only using the 1:1 devices for your tiered reading intervention? Perhaps you are only using the 1:1 devices for math because you have adaptive math software, or you are not in a district that has adopted 1:1 devices yet; you will explain that here.

It could be that in your elementary PreK-2 classrooms you have five iPads. In this case, then maybe you follow a blended station rotation model, where students in small groups work in centers throughout the day using the iPads. In high school, you may have multiple laptop carts rather than a 1:1 scenario. How will you prioritize the use of these machines? If you are not 1:1, you may need to define how you will provide access and equity to students who do not have personal devices, should you be working 100% remotely.

School Level-Implementation

Now that they know the what, discuss the "how". How will the teachers implement this new learning model? How will instructional strategies be different from what stakeholders are familiar? In this section I suggest including detail about specific software the school is providing for teachers to use with students. Give the title of each one by grade and two-three sentences about how each will be used. Call out any professional development the teachers have had to prepare them for the implementation of the new teaching methodology and to become familiar with the new software or applications they are adopting.

For example, did the English department meet in professional learning communities (PLC) to prepare to implement new teaching strategies such as grading essays online and giving digital feedback? Are they using TurnItIn in order to avoid plagiarism? Did they receive training on this?

Make sure to include the definition of plagiarism and PLC. Not many parents know what meeting as a professional learning community is, but several would like to know that essays would be red flagged if their child (or if they) copied and pasted them from the Internet.

Explain what 1:1 will actually look like in classrooms and describe the implementation plan. Another great informational component of the plan for this section is to explain what it will look like at home should you have to transition to remote or simply as a comparison. This will be helpful to your teachers as well. For example:

Time	Classroom Activity	Remote Activity
20 minutes	Independent Reading	Independent Reading
5 minutes	Quizlet Vocabulary Flashcards	Quizlet Flashcards
20 minutes	Compare/Contrast Venn Diagram on teacher provided paper	Compare/Contrast Venn Diagram on SeeSaw
10 minutes	Vocabulary Quiz on SeeSaw	Vocabulary Quiz on SeeSaw
1 hour	Specialties	Art—YouTube, PE—YouTube (or outside)

Will the school begin handing out devices on the first day back to school? Should parents expect their children to bring their devices home? If school begins remotely, this would be a great location to link the schedule for students to pick up their devices. Be certain to link any required paperwork here as well.

Engagement

One of the primary goals of digital instruction is to allow for student-led learning. The teacher should be in the role of a facilitator since the technology allows for a personalized learning pathway based on the student's individualized needs. As a result, learning looks very different to all stakeholders than previously. This may be uncomfortable at first. It is critical to communicate this to stakeholders. Therefore, in the school-level plan is an opportunity to present what you, as the school-level administrator, envision as engagement.

It will be necessary to make stakeholders aware that engagement in digital learning isn't completing worksheets or a lack thereof. It is a focus on higher-order thinking and personalized opportunities to create, apply, and evaluate. Depending on the grade levels within your school, you may decide to include examples of engagement and explain how each example is more motivational to children than when everyone is reading the same page in a textbook together.

Social Media

It is essential that you determine how you want to handle social media as well as third-party sites that are not software as a service (SaaS) in your school-wide implementation plan for digital learning. I highly recommend a committee to approve the use of new of social media or digital communication within the classroom.

Additionally, unless your legal division advises differently, I suggest that you include something similar to the following if it does not already exist in your employee handbook as well.

> *Teachers may only include pictures of students whose parents/guardians have signed the photo release form, and they may only post images of students on sites that require a user ID and password available only to families. Families must be required to opt-in to the opportunity for the digital community, where pictures of students are posted.*

It would be advantageous to provide each teacher with an opt-in form for all school approved social media sites.

Using social media can be a great way to build community in a remote setting and thereby build the communication bridge between parents, students, and teachers, but it can also be like opening Pandora's box. Therefore, you will want to offer some additional communication guidelines in your School-Level Communication Plan for Digital Learning for teachers.

For example, at the district level, teachers are expected to use professional judgement when contacting students through social media. Many students and parents will "add" teachers via social media, especially if school is remote. This adds to their interaction and creates a stronger rapport. For older students, teachers may see concerning behavior on student social media accounts and vice versa. This may also be the case with parents of students. What is the district policy on interacting via social media? Teachers may be afraid to not accept "requests" from social media from certain members of the community. However, if the 2022 communication plan for digital learning states that teachers should not fraternize with students or parents of current students on social media other than school approved accounts, then teachers can use the plan as a reference. This would, therefore, leave them with the option of declining and referencing the communication plan for digital learning. A statement such as this would still allow families to build rapport and create a bridge based on a specific platform that only current families who have opted into have access.

It is common to see guidance around messaging in this section of a communication plan for digital learning. Parents appreciate seeing the guidance provided, and teachers appreciate the specific guidance. For example, do you want to state that direct communication should be age appropriate and specific to the student's education? Do you want to require that parents be copied on all communication to elementary and middle school students, unless parents opt-out? You will see some plans that do not require parents of high school age students to opt-out of receiving copies of communications from teachers, but I strongly suggest you require this.

Internet Safety Policy

I suggest linking to the Devices section of the District-Wide Communications Plan for Digital Learning. Stakeholders will find links to the Acceptable Use Policy, the Internet Safety Policy, Device Acceptance and Insurance policies etc.... there. Students will need to submit all of these before they can receive a device and before logging into the schools Internet.

Discipline

The schools' discipline policy as it relates to theft or loss of equipment, plagiarism, cheating, etc.... will need to be posted in this section. Because the policy should be different based on grade band, this is typically defined at the school-level.

Resources/Accessibility

Your school may choose to list additional resources that are available to students. For example, are there digital library resources available if students are working remotely? Do parents also have access to the student software listed previously? Each vendor with whom you work should provide accessibility requirements. These could be linked by title in this section, along with contact information for any question around accessibility or accommodations.

FAQ

It is best practice for any organization to provide a frequently asked questions (FAQ) section of any plan or interaction with the community. It is also critical that you have several stakeholders read the plan and the FAQ to make sure you avoid education jargon. It is likely that you will have several team members contribute to this plan, and you will want one person to edit it so that the plan reads with a consistent voice.

Plan Location and Formatting

Please note the literacy level of your community when writing your plan. If your school community has an average of a 7th grade literacy level, then a plan written at the 12th grade level doesn't serve much of a purpose. It is critical that the formatting of the document be easy to navigate and that it is located in an easy to identify and locate place on your website. Additionally, the user should be able to click on a teacher's name to view the teacher's Classroom Communication Plan for Digital Learning.

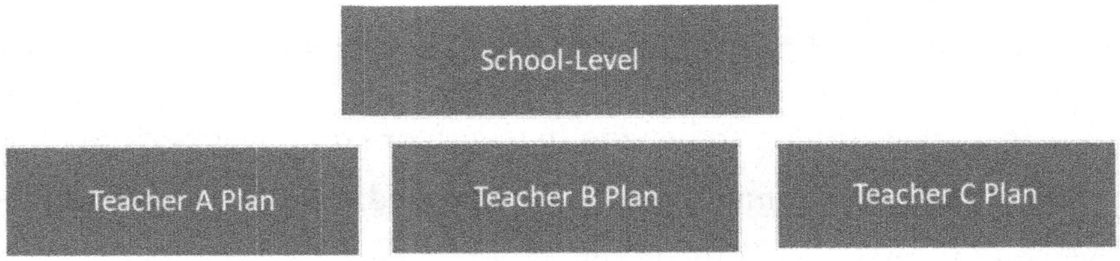

CLASSROOM COMMUNICATION PLAN FOR DIGITAL LEARNING

The Classroom Communication Plan for Digital Learning sets the expectation for students and parents based on the individual teachers planning in alignment with the school-level and district-wide communication plans for digital learning. The goal of the classroom communication plan is to outline all procedures that are necessary to create a bridge of communication between the classroom stakeholders and the individual teacher. In other words, this is where the practitioner side of the pedal meets the medal. This is where the magic happens.

Stakeholders

It is critical that you, as the classroom teacher, define who your stakeholders are as you develop your Classroom Communication Plan for Digital Learning. This way you will know who your audience is and can adjust as needed.

It seems obvious that students are your stakeholders, as are parents, but often times it is easy to overlook that a grandparent may be a primary stakeholder. In these cases, it is important to remember that a grandparent may not be as familiar or as comfortable with technology as a parent or an aunt or an uncle. Also, just because someone's age falls in a range that might make him or her seem like he or she should be technically savvy, that isn't necessarily the case. For this reason, this section of your plan should be made up of a survey for parent/guardians.

The survey doesn't have to be long in length or fancy. It is perfectly fine to make this a questionnaire that is paper-based. Include questions that give you information on the following topics:

- *Do the students and parents have internet access at home?*
- *If there is no access at home, is there somewhere convenient they can get online consistently?*
- *Is there a printer at home that consistently works?*
- *Is there a device at home besides a phone on which to do schoolwork or for the parent/guardian to check grades/email?*

- *Does the parent/guardian regularly check email?*
- *Does the parent/guardian have a smartphone?*
- *Does the parent/guardian have an email address? What is it? Is it checked regularly?*
- *On a scale of 1-10 how tech-savvy do they view themselves?*

Note: Most of the questions require yes/no response or are on a scale. The goal is for your stakeholders to return these and in a timely fashion. You also don't want to intimidate anyone by asking for questions that require in-depth explanations or take a great deal of time.

Implementation Model

In the Classroom Communication Plan for Digital Learning, the classroom implementation model will need to go into more detail than the school-wide implementation model did, but it definitely doesn't need to be an education methods class. Remember, your audience is made up of students, parents, grandparents, aunts, and uncles. They want to know how you are going to use computers and the internet to teach in a way that is better than the way that they learned. What benefit is there for you, as the classroom teacher, the expert in instruction, to use this type of instructional model? As a result of the technology, will you be able to look at data every Wednesday (formative assessments) and from practice activities they did Tuesday after your instruction on Monday? Then will you reteach before the test on Friday?

In this section I suggest outlining how you plan to use Carnegie Math, for example, for your response to intervention tool (don't forget to explain what RTI is), but explain how you also plan to come up with real-world applications of the math concepts based on children's interests. Then you plan to have the children create career projects based on online research, or perhaps you plan to use an online site where the child can simulate cutting right triangles for laying carpet in order to apply Geometry to the real-world. These real-world connections are what engage students. If the class is working remotely, parents would appreciate this online activity over their child trying to cut up their living room carpet.

Another example you might give if you are studying *Rome and Juliet* is how you plan to use virtual reality. Perhaps you plan to have the children perform the balcony scene through virtual reality, where they take on the role of either Rome or Juliet repeating the lines of whichever respective character is appropriate, while being fully immersed in the play. This section of the plan is your chance to highlight your creativity and how you are embracing the benefits of the technology, while highlighting your expertise and passion for your subject area.

Specifically, you could describe that even with social distancing during the Covid-19 pandemic or even though students are not physically together because maybe one of your students is travelling for competitions, another of your students is hospital homebound, and other students are homeschool for a variety of reasons, you are actually more capable of having students work productively in groups if they do so online rather than in person. Therefore, you plan to have them complete their weekly lab questions online, regardless of whether they are at school or working from home.

In other words, in this section, give an overview of your implementation model.

- *A day in my classroom...*

Because some parents will still struggle with conceptualizing with what a digital classroom looks like, it will be helpful to make a schedule or write a description of what it might be like to be in your classroom. This will look different, of course, whether you are elementary, middle, or high school.

Example:

A Day In My Online Classroom Sample Activity Instructions: Everything you read online is true, right? Today we are going to see what you remember about Christopher Columbus. In your online class you have a document with two columns, one for the Truth and one for Lies. List four truths and four lies that you find on the AllAboutExplorers.com website.

Time	Classroom	Remote
10 min.	Turn in HW, Journal	Journal, snack
15 min.	AllAboutExplorers.com	AllAboutExplorers.com
15 min.	Complete Truth/Lie	Complete Truth/Lie
10 min.	Debrief in groups	Debrief in groups

Rules

If you are meeting face-to-face, you will need to define how you will hold the children accountable for bringing their devices not only to class but also for bringing them to class charged as well. Will you give them a participation grade each day?

If they are remote, what happens when they log in late, or what happens if they didn't charge their machine the night before and therefore cannot log in on time? Remember, not bringing a charged device to class is like showing up with no textbook or paper or pencils. Make sure to consult with the district-wide or school-level policies on tardiness and attendance. Since some parents may need assistance with child-care when schools are remote, there may be flexibility needed for tardiness or attendance.

You will, however, definitely want to address digital citizenship and have procedures in place for social interaction. Cyber-bullying is incredibly common. The anonymity the computer screen provides does not work to bring out the best in all children or adults, for that matter. Consider having the children sign a pledge of social respect before they interact in your digital classroom.

Often times, they don't realize how something comes across in writing without their award-winning personalities or smiles to support it. Unfortunately, this is often a hard lesson learned.

Spending time on this initially will definitely be worth it for you and other children, especially if you plan to have the learners interact in discussion forums or through peer editing.

You will want to consult the School-Level Communication Plan for Digital Learning on discipline regarding plagiarism and online cheating as you design your tiers for discipline on these topics, for this will likely come up, especially with older students. I'd suggest hyperlinking to this section of the school-level plan as well as listing your initial steps of discipline. For example, what happens when you get an email like the following:

> *Could you please tell me how to unsubmit an assignment or can you delete assignments for a student? It is urgent!!! Pretty Please!! I did work for someone and they don't wanna pay me. I need everything deleted immediately. Please help me.*

This is an actual email I received. Of course, both students were disciplined. It is better to plan in advance how to handle issues with academic integrity than to get caught off guard. Most cheating attempts would not pass an intelligence test, so they aren't hard to determine. You will also need to answer questions from many skeptical parents about cheating. How do you know if a child is cheating? In truth, you know the same way you do in a traditional classroom. If you know your students, then you know the level of work they are capable of doing. Authentic assessments make it difficult to cheat. Live lessons where students interact or meetings during office hours also help teachers to identify student capability.

Just like in a traditional classroom, you should expect students be engaged and present, but you will want to communicate that in your classroom plan. Otherwise stakeholders may not recognize the commonality in the mediums. Likewise, they may not realize that if students are remote, expecting them to log into live lessons daily or checking email daily is equivalent to attending class in person. Therefore, it is necessary to specify your expectations very clearly in your classroom plan. Just like you expect students to attend face-to-face class five days a week, you expect students to attend online five days a week when they are working remotely, unless of course the online course is set up to be an asynchronous online course where students work at their own pace. Stakeholders, of course, won't know this if it isn't communicated.

Communication

Because stakeholders, to include students, are not used to interacting with a teacher digitally, you will want to tell them your preferred method of communication. For example, do you prefer to be messaged via email or do you prefer a telephone call? Many will even want to text message you.

It isn't uncommon to see guidance around messaging in this section of a communication plan for digital learning. Parents appreciate seeing the guidance provided, and most teachers appreciate the specific guidance. You will want to investigate the requirements of your school. For example, is there a requirement that parents be copied on all communication to elementary and middle school students, unless parents opt-out? You will see some plans that do not require parents of high school age students to opt-out of receiving copies of communications from teachers, but I strongly suggest you require this. Requesting stakeholders opt out of this communication option is something you could include in your stakeholder survey. A teacher can never over-communicate about a student's performance.

It is critical to encourage two-way communication with stakeholders. One way to do that is to manage expectations on the turn-around time for communication. For example, in this section of the plan, make stakeholders aware of your timelines for grading and for responding to communication requests. Also, from what email address or phone numbers should they expect to see a response from you?

This consistency will encourage them to reply to you. Other ways you can encourage communication is by sending weekly newsletters that included your plans for the week so that stakeholders constantly feel as though they are on the same page with you as far as planning. Within the newsletter, you can provide weekly questions to discuss with the children that relate to the work. While parents may not have textbooks to reference, your weekly questions will give them talking points to share with their children.

Plan Location and Formatting

Remember, this is not your class syllabus, nor should it include every detail about your class. This plan should be specifically about the digital learning that will take place in your classroom. If you know the specific resources associated with projects that you will use throughout the year, then you can include a chart to list them for stakeholders, but any additional detail would need to be added to a class syllabus. It will be critical to link this plan to your school-level communication plan for digital learning.

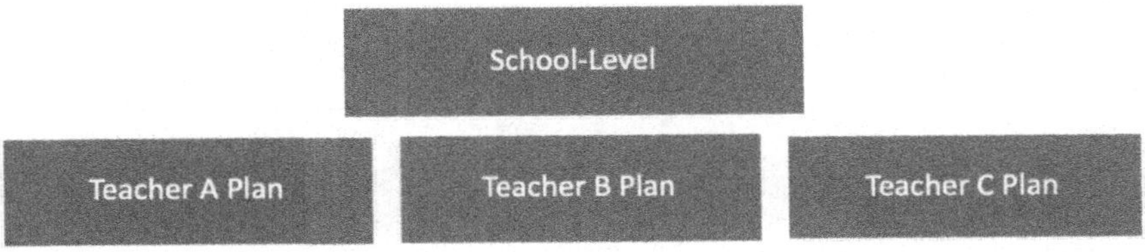

REFERENCES

- 51 Critical Cyber-bullying Statistics in 2019. *Broadband Search*. Retrieved from: www.broadbandsearch.net/blog/cyber-bullying-statistics

- Anderson, M., & Jiang, J. (2018, May). "Teens, social media, & technology." *Pew Research Center Internet & Technology.* Retrieved from: www.pewinternet.org/2018/05/31/teens-social-media-technology-2018/

- Asselin, S. B., & Mooney, M. (1996). *Diverse learners: Strategies for success.* Virginia Vocational Curriculum and Resource Center. (406-529)

- Auxier, B., Anderson, M. Perrin, A. & Turner, E. (2020, July 28) "Parenting children in the age of screens." Pew Research Center. Retrieved from www.pewresearch.org/internet/2020/07/28/parenting-children-in-the-age-of-screens/

- Bergman, P. & Chan, E. (2019). Leveraging parents through low cost technology: The impact of high-frequency information on student achievement. *The Journal of Human Resources, 51*(1), 125-158. https://doi.org/10.3368/jhr.56.1.1118-9837R1

- Braiker, B. (2013). High-tech kids: Are they really smarter? *Parenting, 27*, 66-68.

- Brown, P. C., Roediger, H. L., & McDaniel, M. A. (2014). *Make it stick: The science of successful Learning*. The Belknap Press of Harvard University Press.

- Carr, N. (2011). *The shallows: What the internet is doing to our brains*. W. W. Norton & Company.

- Chappuis, J., Stiggins, R., Chappuis, S., & Arter, J. (2012). *Classroom assessment for student learning: Doing it right—using it well.* Pearson.

- Child Rescue Network. (2019). *Internet Safety. Enough Is Enough: Making the Internet Safer for Children and Families*. Retrieved from: www.enough.org/stats_internet safety

- Child Rescue Network. (2019). *Internet Safety*. Retrieved from: http://childrescuenetwork.org/keeping-children-safe/internet-safety/

- Christensen, C., Johnson, C. W., & Horn, M. B. (2008). *Disrupting class: How disruptive innovation will change the way the world learns*. McGraw-Hill.

- Common core standards initiative: preparing America's students for college and career. (2018, August) Retrieved from: www.corestandards.org/about-the-standards/development-process/

- Coomey, M., & Stephenson, J. (2001). Online learning: It's all about dialogue, involvement, support and control—according to the research. In J. Stephenson (Ed.), Teaching and learning online (pp. 37-52). London: Kogan Page.

- Cooper, H. (2001). *The battle over homework* (2nd ed.). Corwin Press, Inc.

- Council, B. S. (2018, December 11). Better Sleep Council Research Finds That Too Much Homework Can Actually Hurt Teens' Performance In School. PR Newswire: news distribution, targeting and monitoring. www.prnewswire.com/news-releases/better-sleep-council-research-finds-that-too-much-homework-can-actually-hurt-teens-performance-in-school-300763823.html

- *Cyber Actors Target K-12 Distance Learning Education to Cause Disruptions and Steal Data.* (2020, December 10). Cybersecurity & Infrastructure Security Agency. https://us-cert.cisa.gov/ncas/alerts/aa20-345a

- Dillinger, J. (2018, March). Number of sex offenders by state. *World Atlas*. Retrieved from: www.worldatlas.com/articles/state-by-state-numbers-of-registered-sex-offenders-in-the-us.html

- Dweck, C. S. (2008). *Mindset. The new psychology of success.* Random House Publishing Group.

- Echols, M. E. (2014). American workers are way behind. *Chief Learning Officer, 13*(2), 10.

- Elmore, T. (2012, February 8). A new generation of parents. Retrieved from: www.howtolearn.com/2012/02/a-new-generation-of-parents/

- Edsurge. (2014, April). *Scrutinizing data privacy policies of Edmodo, Khan, and Pearson*. Retrieved October 15, 2020, from: www.edsurge.com/n/2014-04-14-scrutinizing-data-privacy-policies-of-edmodo-khan-and-pearson

- Fedock, B. & Young, E. (2013). Rethinking Online Writing and Communication Skills as a Process: Teaching Skills through Interactive, Learning Style Based Modeling. In R. McBride & M. Searson (Eds.), *Proceedings of SITE 2013—Society for Information Technology & Teacher Education International Conference,* 1291—1297. Association for the Advancement of Computing in Education (AACE). Retrieved December 31, 2020 from: www.learntechlib.org/primary/p/48302/.

- Fedock, B., & Young, E. (2013). Rethinking online writing and communication skills as a process: Teaching skills through interactive, learning style-based modeling. *Society for Information Technology & Teacher Education International Conference, 13*(1), *1291-1297.*

- Florence, F., & Hamilton, M. L. (2018). No more pencils, no more books: A district digital conversion. EdSurge (www.edsurge.com/n/2014-04-30-no-more-pencils-no-more-books-a-district-digital-conversion). Retrieved July 1, 2019.

- Formative Instructional Practices (n.d.) Retrieved February 01, 2021, from www.cgcatogo.com/uploads/1/0/6/7/10675379/module_3_section_1_activity_2.pdf

- Ghose, T. (2016, October). Pediatricians: No more than 2 hours screen time daily for kids. *Scientific American*. Retrieved from:

www.scientificamerican.com/article/pediatricians-no-more-than-2-hour-screen-time-kids/

- Grisham, D. L., & Wolsey, T.D. (2006). Re-centering the middle school classroom as a vibrant learning community: Students, literacy, and technology intersect. *Journal of Adult and Adolescent Literacy, 49*(8), 648-660.

- Hamlin, C. & Voelker, C. (2020, December 16, 2020). Personal Interview.

- Hattie, J. (2009). *Visible Learning: A synthesis of over 800 Meta-Analyses Relating to Achievement.* Routledge Taylor & Francis Group.

- Hess, K. (2004). Applying Webb's depth-of-knowledge levels in reading. [online] available: www.nciea.org

- Horn, B., & Staker, H. (2014). *Blended: Using disruptive innovation to improve schools.* Jossey-Bass.

- Jenson, F. E., & Nutt, A. E. (2016). *The teenage brain: A neuroscientist's survival guide to raising adolescents and young adults.* HarperCollins.

- Kanj, M., & Mitic, W. (2009). Health literacy and health promotion: Definitions, concepts and examples in the Eastern Mediterranean region. Retrieved from: www.gchp7.info/resources/downloads/t1.pdf

- Kinash, S., Wood, K., & Knight, D. (2013). "Digital immigrant teachers and digital native students: What happens to teaching?,"

Learning and Teaching Papers Paper, 50. Retrieved from: http://epublications.bond.edu.au/tls/50

- Kotchick, B. A., & Forehand, R. (2002). Putting parenting in perspective: A discussion of the contextual factors that shape parenting practices. *Journal of Child and Family Studies, 11*(3), 255-269.

- Lenhart, A. (2007, June). Cyberbullying and Online Teens. Pew Research Center & Internet Technology. Retrieved from: www.pewinternet.org/2007/06/27/cyberbullying

- Lenhart, A. (2009, December). Teens and sexting. *Pew Research Center & Internet Technology*. Retrieved from: www.pewinternet.org/2009/12/15/teens-and-sexting.

- Lenhart, A. (2010, February). Social media and young adults. *Pew Research Center Internet & Technology.* Retrieved from: www.pewinternet.org/2010/02/03/social-media-and-young-adults/

- Levin, D., & Arafeh, S. (2002). The digital disconnect: The widening gap between internet-savvy students and their schools. *Washington, DC: Pew Internet & American Life Project,* August 14, 2002. Report, 67, 20. Retrieved from: www.pewinternet.org/~/media/Files/Reports/2002/PIP_Schools_Internet_Report.pdf.pdf

- Lock, J., Eaton, SE., & Kessy, E. (2017. "Fostering self-regulation in online learning in K-12 education," *Northwest Journal of Teacher Education*: Vol. 12: Iss. 2, Article2. DOI: 10.15760/nwjte.2017.12.2.2

- Meyer, C. D., Farmer, S., Nara, F., & Azim-khan, R., (2019, June 3). *Countdown to CCPA:2 GDPR Compliance Does Not Equal*

CCPA Compliance. Pillsbury. Retrieved from: www.pillsburylaw.com/en/news-and-insights/ccpa-compliance-gdpr.html

- Miller, M. (2011, October, 5). *Understanding Generation Z: The Facebook generation.* Retrieved from: www.quepublishing.com/articles/article.aspx?p=1753977

- National Forum on Educational Statistics, (2006). *Forum guide to elementary/secondary education* (NFES 2006-803). Washington, DC: U.S. Department of Education, National Forum on Education Statistics.

- NCAA Eligibility Center. (2020, January 27). *NCAA eligibility requirements*. Retrieved from https://web3.ncaa.org/ecwr3/

- Organization for Economic Cooperation and Development (2012), *Literacy, Numeracy and Problem Solving in Technology-Rich Environments: Framework for the OECD Survey of Adult Skills.* OECD Publishing. https://doi.org/10.1787/9789264128859-en

- Oliver, W. L. (2010). "Investigating whether a value-added teaching effectiveness model designed for traditional classrooms can be used to measure online teaching quality." (Doctoral Dissertation). Available from Proquest Dissertations and Theses database. (UMI No. 851893465). https://scholar.utc.edu/theses/353

- Oliver, W. (2014). Oliver's framework for online instruction. Retrieved January 29, 2021: from https://blendedpractice.com/framework/

- Parker, K. & Igielnik, R. (2020). On the cusp of adulthood and facing an uncertain future: what we know about Gen Z so far. Pew

Research Center: Social & Demographic Trends. Retrieved from https://www.pewsocialtrends.org/essay/on-the-cusp-of-adulthood-and-facing-an-uncertain-future-what-we-know-about-gen-z-so-far/

- Parr, B. (2010, October). "The average teenager sends 3,339 texts per month STATS." *Mashable*. Retrieved from: https://mashable.com/2010/10/14/nielsen-texting-stats/#PTJrTxmueSqz

- Patchin, J.W. & Hinduja, S. (2019) It is time to teach safe sexting. Journal of Adolescent Health, 66(2), 140-143. https://doi.org/10.1016/j.jadohealth.2019.10.010

- Paton, G. (2014, April). Infant unable to use toy building blocks due to iPad addiction. *The Telegraph*. Retrieved from: http://www.telegraph.co.uk/education/educationnews/10767878/Infants-unable-to-use-toy-building-blocks-due-to-iPad-addiction.html

- Powell, A. (2020, November 24, 2020). Personal Interview.

- Quality Matters. (2019). Course Design Rubric Standards. Retrieved October 14, 2020, from: https://www.qualitymatters.org/qa-resources/rubric-standards/k-12-secondary-rubric

- Quality Matters & The Virtual Learning Leadership Alliance. (2019, February 27). The Standards. Retrieved October 14, 2020, from: https://www.nsqol.org/the-standards/

- Rice, K. (2012). *Making the move to K-12 online teaching: Research-based strategies and practices*. Pearson.

- Rideout, V. (2018). *Zero to eight: Children's media use in America*. Common Sense Media. Retrieved from: www.

commonsensemedia.org/sites/default/files/research/zerotoeightfinal2018.pdf

- Rideout, V. M. A. & Robb, M. B. (2018). *Social media, social lives: Teens reveal their experiences.* Common Sense Media. Retrieved from www.commonsensemedia.org/research/social-media-social-life-2018

- Rideout, V., & Robb, M. B. (2020). *The common sense census: Media use by kids age zero to eight, 2020.* Common Sense Media.

- Roblyer, M. D., & Davis, L. (2008). Predicting success for virtual school students: Putting research-based models to practice. *Online Journal of Distance Learning Administration, 11*(4). http://eric.ed.gov/?id=EJ1065647

- Roblyer, M. D., & Doering, A. (2013). *Integrating educational technology into teaching* (6th ed.). Pearson.

- Roizen, M. F., & Oz, M. C. (2010). *You raising your child.* Simon & Schuster, Inc.

- Rozario, B. (2011, April 4). *How to parent Gen Y and Z.* Retrieved from: http://parenthots.com/features/How-to-parent-Gen-Y-and-Z.aspx

- Russel, L. (2020, December 15, 2020). Personal Interview.

- Sales, N. J. (2016). *American girls, social media and the secret lives of teenagers.* Penguin Random House.

- Savery, J. (2014). Be VOCAL: Characteristics of successful online instructors. *Journal of Interactive Online Learning, 4*(2). www.ncolr.org/jiol/issues/pdf/4.2.6.pdf. ISSN: 1541-4914

- Schroer, W. (2004, April 16). Generations X, Y, Z and the others. *The Social Librarian*. Retrieved from: www.socialmarketing.org/newsletter/features/generation3.htm

- Seaman, J. E., Allen, J. I., Seaman, J. (2018). Grade increase: Tracking distance education in the United States. Babson Survey Research Group. Retrieved from: www.onlinelearningsurvey.com/reports/gradeincrease.pdf

- Sen, B. (2009, May 23). The relationship between frequency of family dinner and adolescent problem behaviors after adjusting for other family characteristics. *Journal of Adolescence*. https://www.sciencedirect.com/science/article/abs/pii/S0140197109000372?via=ihub

- Sheninger, E.C. & Murray, T.C. (2017). *Learning transformed: 8 keys to designing tomorrow's schools, today.* Alexandria, VA: Association for Supervision and Curriculum Development.

- Shuler, C. (2012). *iLearn II: An analysis of the education category of the iTunes App Store.* New York: The Joan Ganz Cooney Center at Sesame Workshop.

- SimpleK12.com. *Practical Online Teacher Training.* Retrieved December 23, 2020 from https://www.SimpleK12.com/practical-online-teacher-training/. Accessed 23 December 2020.

- Smith, S. (2018). *Teacher Evaluation and Effectiveness Report.* Michigan Virtual University. Retrieved from: https://mvlri.org/research/publications/teacher-evaluation-and-effectiveness-report/

- Taylor, M. (2004). Generation NeXT comes to college: Meeting the postmodern student. [Monograph]. Retrieved from: www.lib.wayne.edu/sites/accreditation/examples/documents/generationnext.pdf

- Teaching Online Certificate. (n.d.). Retrieved December 23, 2020, from www.qualitymatters.org/professional-development/toc

- Travis, S. (2020). Teen sex act used to videobomb virtual school class. Retrieved October 15, 2020 from: www.sun-sentinel.com/news/education/fl-ne-student-sex-video- mcarthur-high-20200918-xgvpq4gvarbyhkleicv4c3vkd4-story.html

- United States National Commission on Excellence in Education. (1983). A nation at risk: The imperative for educational reform: A report to the Nation and the Secretary of Education, United States Department of Education. Washington, D.C.: The Commission: [Supt. of Docs., U.S. G.P.O. distributor].

- Usdan, J., & Almasy, K. (2012). FCC Chairman Announces Jobs-Focused Digital Literacy Partnership Between Connect2Compete and the 2,800 American Job Centers. Retrieved from: www.fcc.gov/news-events/blog/2012/07/23/fcc-chairman-announces-jobs-focused-digital-literacy-partnership-between

- Walsh, F., Branham, D., & Payne, S. (2013). *Are generational differences in the workplace driving you nuts?* Proceedings of the American Correctional Association Conference, Houston, TX.

Retrieved from: www.aca.org/conferences/winter2013/WC2013_Presentations/B-4A%20Are%20Generational%20Differences%20in%20the%20Workplace%20Driving%20You%20Nuts.pdf

- Watson, J. (2018, September 27). *Welcome to the Digital Learning Collaborative!* Retrieved December 23, 2020, from: www.digitallearningcollab.com/blog/2018/9/27/welcome-to-the-digital-learning-collaborative

- Weinberger, J. W. (2017). *The boogeyman exists: And he's in your child's back pocket* (2nd ed.). Self-Published, Weinberger.